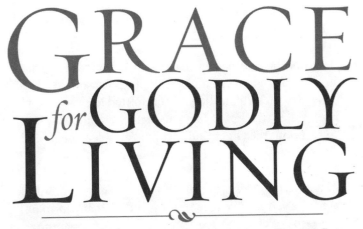

GRACE for GODLY LIVING

ALLOWING GOD'S GRACE TO PRODUCE A GODLY LIFE

PAUL CHAPPELL

First published in 2005 by Striving Together Publications, a ministry of Lancaster Baptist Church, Lancaster, CA 93535. Striving Together Publications is committed to providing tried, trusted, and proven books that will further equip local churches to carry out the Great Commission. Your comments and suggestions are valued.

Striving Together Publications
4020 E. Lancaster Blvd.
Lancaster, CA 93535
800.201.7748

Typed by Julie Jenkins
Edited by Cary Schmidt
Cover design by Daniel Irmler
Layout by Craig Parker

ISBN 978-1-59894-080-0

Printed in the United States of America

Table of Contents

Dedication

This book is dedicated to the servant leaders of Lancaster Baptist Church. Your ministry of faithfulness to teach, witness, and serve is a blessing every day! Thank you for growing in the grace of godly living and for setting an example of Christian faithfulness for the generations to follow us!

Preface

Grace for Godly Living is a collection of Bible studies delivered to the Lancaster Baptist Church during the 1990s. During these foundational years, it was our desire not to merely mandate outward conformity, but to nurture Christians in their growth process, so that they might "do the will of God from the heart."

This study was meant to help a young church grow in the grace of godliness. It has been requested for years in book form. We pray it will encourage the readers.

Introduction

As our American culture moves quickly toward a post-modern society, it seems the key doctrine of the hour is, "Whatever is good for you is okay."

This "whatever" philosophy is running rampant in church life and in Christian homes due to the conformity of churches to this world's culture.

As Bible-believing Christians, we must remember, it is not the duty of the church to adapt Christ to men, but to adapt men to Christ.

Strangely, as the spirit of this world is seen more and more in the lives of some believers, the claims of these dear people is that they have grace to live the way they want to live. Somehow a philosophy of grace, that is often in opposition to scriptural principles, is fueling the fire of Christians who want to live a "have it your way" brand of the Christian life.

Furthermore, many of the proponents of this type of grace teaching want to claim that Christians with more conservative and biblically-based guidelines for living do not understand "grace." It seems many Christ-honoring and loving pastors are now viewed as the great "kill-joys" of the twenty-first century. Apparently, the conservative Christian may not use his liberty to teach and practice the lifestyle he believes to be honoring to the Lord.

Tragically, in the evangelical-fundamental world there has developed a philosophy similar to the liberal politics of the day. A philosophy that teaches tolerance and grace, but has become extremely intolerant of ministries whose worship styles or lifestyles are a few decades (or millennia) behind the modern church.

Yes, there have been pastors and spiritual leaders who have not properly emphasized the Scripture's teachings with a spirit of love. Yes, many conservative Christians need a renewal of the joy of the Holy Spirit in their lives, but the broad-brushed picture being painted against all conservative ministries is not accurate.

There are still thousands of churches in the land who believe the grace of God will produce a distinctive fruit in the spiritual wasteland of our day. We believe America needs to see in us a worship and lifestyle that is not a rerun of a late-night show.

Wherever one sides on these issues, it is a truth from Scripture, that a Spirit-controlled Christian will evidence a loving spirit in their relationships with others. It is not a good policy to preach grace while involved in hurtful slander of a fellow believer.

The following pages reflect one pastor's attempt to scripturally define grace, and to describe the effect of it in the life of a believer. It is my prayer that these thoughts may be used by the Lord to strengthen lives to the glory of God.

PART ONE

Disciplined by Grace

CHAPTER ONE

Defining Grace

Moreover the law entered, that the offence might abound. But where sin abounded, grace did much more abound: That as sin hath reigned unto death, even so might grace reign through righteousness unto eternal life by Jesus Christ our Lord. What shall we say then? Shall we continue in sin, that grace may abound? God forbid. How shall we, that are dead to sin, live any longer therein? Know ye not, that so many of us as were baptized into Jesus Christ were baptized into his death? Therefore we are buried with him by baptism into death: that like as Christ was raised up from the dead by the glory of the Father, even so we also should walk in newness of life. For if we have been planted together in the likeness of his death, we shall be also in the likeness of his resurrection: Knowing this, that our old man is crucified with him, that the body of sin might be destroyed, that henceforth we should not serve sin. For he that is dead is freed from sin. Now if we be dead with Christ, we believe that we shall also live with him: Knowing that Christ being raised from the dead dieth no more; death hath no more dominion over him. For in that he died, he died unto sin once: but in that he liveth, he liveth unto God. Likewise reckon ye also yourselves to be dead indeed unto sin, but alive unto God through Jesus Christ our Lord. Let not sin therefore reign in your mortal body, that ye should obey it in the lusts thereof. Neither yield ye your members as instruments of unrighteousness unto sin: but yield yourselves unto God, as those that are alive from the dead, and your members as instruments of righteousness unto God. For sin shall not have dominion over you: for ye are not under the law, but under grace. What then? shall we sin, because we are not under the law, but under grace? God forbid. Know ye not, that to whom ye yield yourselves servants to obey, his servants ye are to whom ye obey; whether of sin unto death, or of obedience unto righteousness?—Romans 5:20–6:16

In December 1980, my wife Terrie and I were married in San Jose, California. As we stood in the reception line on our wedding day, folks came by to greet us and give us various wedding gifts. Over the next few days, we opened those gifts and began to see how folks had expressed their love to us. There was one little box that I opened, and inside was a gift from my grandmother. That gift was a book entitled *Disciplined by Grace*. I opened the book, and on the inside it said,

> *Dear Paul and Terrie,*
>
> *This is one of the best books you will ever read. Be sure your family understands this book. I love you so much.*
>
> *Grandmother*

Recently, as I read through the book again, I could not help but notice the contrast between this book, written over fifty years ago, and recent philosophies, materials, and broadcasts which have been coming forth concerning the subject of grace. What a tremendously different approach to grace we see from fifty years ago to this day.

Differing Philosophies of Grace

As I read *Disciplined by Grace* again recently, I noticed that the subtitle was, "Studies in Christian Conduct." The differing philosophies about grace in this day and age do not primarily revolve around the subject of salvation by grace when it concerns Christian people. Most people, if they are truly Christian, will agree that salvation is totally by God's grace and through faith. The area of great difference, however, seems to come in the realm of sanctification. I believe the Bible teaches that a proper understanding of grace will affect Christian conduct and will cause me to become more sanctified in my everyday life.

Sanctification is the theme of Romans 6. Christians, who are truly born-again, believe salvation is wholly of grace. We believe that when we are saved by grace, we are instantly justified before a holy God. After justification, we begin to learn about sanctification in the Christian life. Sanctification deals with a process whereby I am separated unto God.

Justification and sanctification take place at the moment of salvation, but sanctification also has a progressive nature whereby I am becoming more mature and more like Jesus Christ. Justification removes the guilt and the penalty of sin. When you were justified, God forgave your sin—the penalty was removed. Sanctification removes the growth and the power of sin.

Romans 6 is a pivotal passage dealing with the subject of grace. In fact, you cannot study grace without coming to Romans 6. However, this chapter is primarily a discourse on the holy life of the believer. I want you to fix that in your mind. Romans 6 is not primarily about grace, but it is primarily about what grace produces in a person's life. Grace will always produce holiness or sanctification unto God.

> *But now being made free from sin, and become servants to God, ye have your fruit unto holiness, and the end everlasting life.*—Romans 6:22

You and I must beware of any teaching of grace which de-emphasizes holy living. There are two schools of thought about grace. The biblical school of thought maintains that as you grow in God's grace, you will be disciplined to live a life that is more Christ-like. The Bible says it is possible to live a life that grieves the Holy Spirit. But by God's grace it is also possible to live a life that pleases Him.

> *Thou therefore endure hardness, as a good soldier of Jesus Christ. No man that warreth entangleth himself with the affairs of this life; that he may please him who hath chosen him to be a soldier.*—2 Timothy 2:3-4

Then there is the new concept of grace, which teaches the idea of having your way in the Christian life. Teachings about grace which de-emphasize righteous living have snared many Christians in the past, and many people in churches today are being influenced by false doctrines about grace. These teachings often view grace as a form of license to live according to one's own will. People who sit in good churches are exposed to this new thought about grace through the radio and bookstores. This often becomes a stumbling block and a hindrance to their walk of progressive sanctification. There are no new tricks in the Devil's bag. This problem of misusing and misunderstanding grace goes right back to the first century.

> *For, brethren, ye have been called unto liberty; only use not liberty for an occasion to the flesh, but by love serve one another.*—Galatians 5:13

Someone may say, "Hey, I have liberty to do what I want to do and to go where I want to go!" Paul said, "Wait, you're misunderstanding Christian liberty." If you really understand Christian liberty, you are going to say, "Lord, how can I be a servant to You? Lord, how can I serve someone else?" That is the mature Christian's understanding of Christian liberty.

In recent days I have read from Dr. J. Vernon McGee's notes on Romans 6. In introducing the chapter, he wrote these words: "This section delivers us from the prevalent idea that you can do as you please. Union with Christ means He is Lord and Master."[1] He says Romans 6 has nothing to do with doing as you please; it has everything to do with making Jesus Christ your Lord and your Master.

In these days, many professing Christians not only want freedom to live their way, but they are also resentful toward anyone who espouses the belief that grace should discipline us toward holiness. Someone who teaches that grace should discipline us to a holy life, and someone who will give examples of what holiness is by preaching about certain types of sin, is often misunderstood or misrepresented by people who want their own way.

Many Christians want to define freedom as their license to live the way they want to live. Many times, those who claim to be filled with grace have resorted to referring to conservative churches in very unfriendly terms—the favorite of which is "legalistic." The term "legalist" simply refers to those who add works to salvation. Those who believe that we are disciplined by grace to live a more holy life are sometimes accused of being legalistic. To even suggest something that might be helpful to you in your sanctification with God might also cause others to accuse you of being legalistic.

There are many writers in Christian circles who espouse the "radical grace" teaching. Some, in recent days, become somewhat critical of those of us who believe in the teaching of Romans 6 concerning the sanctification of the believer. Though I believe they are Christians, they are not fundamental, Bible-believing Baptists. They are not fundamentalists by their own admission.

I believe that our fundamental Baptist position is right doctrinally. I do not say that everyone in the fundamental Baptist movement is perfect, and some personalities within our movement have disappointed me. But, I refuse to throw away a right position because of a few wrong personalities. I encourage you to look beyond people to Jesus Christ and to find the right position doctrinally in Him. I encourage you to be in church because you believe the church is standing for the truth.

While many of these modern Christian authors are encouraging and very neutral, they sometimes refer to conservative churches in unkind ways. I once heard a radio teacher refer to people more conservative than himself in the following way. "They are [churches] filled with squint-eyed legalists, grace killers, shamers, religious rigidity, negative, grim, joyless people, frowning saints seated in the pews." They are using words as they comment on the subject of grace that are not very gracious. Those who are proponents of what could be called the "radical grace" teaching, turn the tables when describing conservative evangelicals, or what we might call fundamental churches. While there may be conservative Christians who act this way, it is not fair to characterize them with a broad swipe that affects many Christian people. Their phrases are calculated to prejudice or "marginalize" their readers and listeners against those who disagree with them.

In Dr. Ernest Pickering's book *Are Fundamentalists Legalists?*, he writes concerning a popular author:

> The viewpoint espoused in his book [speaking of a "radical grace" teacher] finds a sympathetic audience with some fundamentalists who have become "bent out of shape" with what they view as the pettiness of certain segments of fundamentalist thinking.[2]

Dr. Pickering says this particular teaching about grace is very appealing to someone who is sitting in a fundamental church and is bent out of shape about something because it becomes a springboard out or a reason or an excuse to live any way one prefers. Instead of saying, "I'd rather attend a church that encourages me to wear shorts to church, or a church that encourages me to watch rated R movies"; it is easier to say, "I'm going to get away from the rigidity, the control, and the repression so I can live the way I want to live."

The proponents of the "radical grace" have spiritualized and found a niche, if you will, with a ready audience of people who believe that it is too hard to live the biblical Christian life. (By the way, it is not too hard if you understand grace.) Even some independent Baptists have fallen for this concept and fallen prey to the "radical grace" teaching.

Why This Attitude toward Fundamental Churches?

I would propose the question, "Why this attitude toward fundamental churches?" Why is this attitude somewhat prevalent in the mainstream "New Evangelical" crowd toward fundamental Christians? (The term "New Evangelical" was coined by Harold Ockenga of Fuller Seminary over forty years ago. It was the term used to bridge the gap between modernists and fundamentalists.)

Factors within Fundamentalism

First of all, some fundamental churches have a lack of balance. They have not properly emphasized love in their churches and their teachings have not been expositional and patient in nature. They have been viewed as all rigidity, all rules, and they have become notorious for that wrong spirit. In most cases, this is a false description of our good, fundamental Baptist churches.

I have spent my life in these churches. I have preached across America in different conservative churches. They are happy, joyful places. In many cases, they are the most red-hot, soulwinning places in the nation where people are getting saved and baptized.

I do not think it is fair to characterize a church that is spending massive amounts of its income, time, and energy to see people saved and encouraged as an unloving church. Unfortunately, in my opinion, some of our fundamental churches have been seen as too rigid and not loving enough. They have not tried to have balance.

The second factor within fundamentalism is that some fundamental churches have lacked a scriptural foundation for their standards of separation. In other words, they just name off these standards but never try to explain them scripturally. This has been something we have tried to do as lovingly and patiently as we can. We have always taught that a standard of separation must be accompanied by a biblical principle.

I remember the first leadership meeting we had at our church. This is our annual time to share requirements for church leaders (not members in general). There were twenty or thirty potential workers there. We tried to present each requirement of a leader from a biblically principled perspective. Some may not agree with our case, but we have tried over the years to give scriptural support for our standards.

Why do we believe that Christians need to be careful about the wickedness of certain movies? Philippians 4:8 says we are to think about things that are pure, right, just, lovely, and so forth.

> *Finally, brethren, whatsoever things are true, whatsoever things are honest, whatsoever things are just, whatsoever things are pure, whatsoever things are lovely, whatsoever things are of good report; if there be any virtue, and if there be any praise, think on these things.*
> —Philippians 4:8

> *I will set no wicked thing before mine eyes: I hate the work of them that turn aside; it shall not cleave to me.*—Psalm 101:3

When we talk about these matters, we have tried to say, "Here is what the Bible says about the matter." So why do people have a bad attitude toward fundamental churches? Perhaps some good men and ladies have not exercised proper patience and love with new Christians. I think, if we are honest, we can sometimes say that our families are not perfect; our church is not perfect; fundamentalism is not perfect; but we are doing the best we can. I think that is all God calls us to do.

Factors Outside Fundamentalism

Why would proponents of the "radical grace" be looking at us and skewing our movement in this biased way? I think there are some factors outside fundamentalism.

The first factor is that the world is becoming more evil. First Peter 4:4 says, "*Wherein they think it strange that ye run not with them to the same excess of riot, speaking evil of you.*" In Matthew 24:12, the Bible says, "*And because iniquity shall abound, the love of many shall wax cold.*" In other words, they are going to think that you are strange if you are not living the way they live.

There is a movement in America called the Church Growth Movement. This movement is teaching pastors that if they want their church to keep growing, they had better become more and more like the world or people are going to turn away. The Church Growth Movement teaches pastors that they should use rock music and should not preach against certain sins. I could give you a dozen articles by pastors who do not use the word "sin" in their preaching. They brag about the fact that they do not use the word "redemption" and other doctrinal terms. The Church Growth Movement is a movement that says, "Hey, we do not want to be so filled with light or salt in our message that we are rejected in this day in which we minister." The world is becoming more evil, and so the church is being more affected by the world than the church is affecting the world.

Second, new evangelical churches are loosening their position to accommodate this changing world. As the world's morals have declined, many churches have lowered their morals to accommodate that change, all under the guise of grace. Those of us who are trying to stay with our scriptural positions are now being referred to as legalistic by some of the generation that taught us the stand that we take. I am talking about men in their sixties who have flip-flopped on these issues in order to accommodate people. The responsibility of the pastor is not to accommodate people; it is not to accommodate the community—it is to please God. We must always make God, not growth, our goal.

Have you ever felt like saying, "Hey, I need more freedom?" If you define freedom as the ability to live contrary to the Scripture, just shake your pastor's hand and say, "Pastor, I love you. I want to go somewhere so I can just relax and kind of kick back." Do not demonize him or the church he pastors. We respect your liberty to go and worship where you can be comfortable. However, we also believe the primary goal of the Christian life is not to please self, but to please Christ. The goal in our church is to conform our lives to Christ. Separation is not the goal; Jesus is the goal.

The third factor outside of fundamentalism is that society is generally in rebellion toward authority. The Bible says in 2 Timothy 3:1–5, "*This know also, that in the last days perilous times shall come. For men shall be lovers of their own selves, covetous, boasters, proud, blasphemers, disobedient to parents, unthankful, unholy, Without natural affection, trucebreakers, false accusers, incontinent, fierce, despisers of those that are good, Traitors, heady, highminded, lovers of pleasures more than lovers of God; Having a form of godliness, but denying the power thereof: from such turn away."* I am finding that people who had authority problems earlier in their lives are the first to rebel against godly authority. I am not talking about authoritarianism. I am not talking about ungodly leadership. I am talking about God's kind of church-given, Christ-honoring authority.

One popular Christian leader has a message entitled, "Grace to Let People Be." Three things are mentioned in the message. He indicates that we need to stop bothering people who like to smoke. Just give them grace to be what they want to be. He also mentions that he used to preach against people who speak in tongues, but that God has convicted him, and now he's just giving them grace to be what they want to be. He also says he used to think that you should only listen to certain kinds of music, but again he says we need to give people grace to be what they want to be.

I am not trying to be mean toward people who smoke, but I am going to preach against it because I *love* people who smoke. I am not against people who speak in tongues; but I am going to preach what the Bible says about it, and the Bible indicates that tongues are not necessary for revelation today. I am going to preach what the Bible says about rock music, and I am not going to give my teenagers "grace to be what they want to be" in that realm. Parents are still commanded to *"train up a child"* and pastors are still commanded to *"reprove, rebuke, and exhort with all longsuffering and doctrine."*

Society is rebelling toward authority. Therefore, one approach is to just give people "grace" to be what they want to be, even if that means letting them live unscripturally.

I want you to discover what it means to be "under grace." You will find that term in Romans 6:15, *"What then? shall we sin, because we are not under the law, but under grace? God forbid."* If I am controlled by grace, will I become more or less holy? More holy. We know we are made holy, justified before God at salvation, but I am talking about progressive sanctification—becoming more like Jesus Christ in our everyday lives.

James 1:25 says, *"But whoso looketh into the perfect law of liberty, and continueth therein, he being not a forgetful hearer, but a doer of the work, this man shall be blessed in his deed."* Are the words *"…the perfect law of liberty…"* a contradiction or can they coexist? Is the Bible the perfect law of liberty? Do these laws, these passages in the Bible, give me liberty to enjoy my life, or are they a form of restrictive bondage? I believe the terms "perfect law" and "liberty" are not contradictory but can coexist or God would not have put them in the same verse.

In this day when grace and liberty are being redefined to a form of license, may we remember that our liberty is a motivation to service, not to selfishness.

CHAPTER TWO

Through Grace I See My Position in Christ

After twenty-five years of being stranded on an island, Joe was finally rescued. As he climbed onto the rescue boat, his rescuers looked back to the shore and noticed three grass huts.

They were curious and asked, "If you were the only one on the island, why did you have three huts?"

Joe said, "Well, one was my house, and one was my church."

"Well, what was the third one?" they asked.

Joe replied, "Oh, that's where I *used* to go to church."

Many people today are tossed to and fro because they fail to find inner peace through their identity in Christ. Often, Christians will blame a church or parent, but this inner turmoil would be present if they lived alone on an island.

If I am under grace, I will know who I am in Christ, and I will identify with Christ. Romans 6:3-4 gives us a picture of this through water baptism, "*Know ye not, that so many of us as were baptized into Jesus Christ were baptized into his death? Therefore we are buried with him by baptism into death: that like as Christ was raised up from the dead by the glory of the Father, even so we also should walk in newness of life."*

I Am Crucified with Christ

Romans 6:6 says , *"Knowing this, that our old man is crucified with him, that the body of sin might be destroyed, that henceforth we should not serve sin."* Verse five says, *"For if we have been planted together in the likeness of his death, we shall be also in the likeness of his resurrection."* If you will understand this principle, it will help you—when Jesus died, you died.

The flesh was crucified at the Cross, and I am crucified with Christ. Galatians 2:20 says, *"I am crucified with Christ: nevertheless I live; yet not I, but Christ liveth in me: and the life which I now live in the flesh I live by the faith of the Son of God, who loved me, and gave himself for me."* Under grace I understand that my flesh was nailed to the Cross, which is my key to victory in this life. We often teach new Christians 1 John 1:9 as their first memory verse, *"If we confess our sins, he is faithful and just to forgive us our sins, and to cleanse us from all unrighteousness."* However, I believe more and more we need to teach new Christians the truth of Romans 6—that we are crucified with Christ. Our old man was defeated on the Cross, and we already have the victory in Christ!

Many Christians, under the guise of "radical grace" teaching, are digging up the old life. They are digging up something that Jesus wants buried. I understand who I am in Christ, and that He alone will make me happy. I can exercise my "freedom" and call it "liberty," but in the long run that won't make me happy if I am not identified with Christ in His death, burial, and resurrection. We are to find our identity in Him. *"For if we have been planted together in the likeness of his death, we shall be also in the likeness of his resurrection"* (Romans 6:5).

I hear of Christians, under the guise of liberty, saying, "Wow! I can do what I want to do. I can dance when I want to dance. I can party with my old friends. I am experiencing liberty." They are not experiencing the Bible's kind of liberty. If you know who you are in Christ, you realize the old life is a crucified life and that the new life is His life. We are resurrected with Christ to a new life!

I Have New Appetites

A saved man can experience new appetites, because a saved man is seated with Him in the heavenlies. Ephesians 2:6 says, *"And hath raised us up together, and made us sit together in heavenly places in Christ Jesus."* The saved man doesn't say, "How can I find a religious reason to go backwards?" A saved man says, "How can I, as I grow in God's grace, learn to be more like Jesus Christ? I have new appetites now. I have new desires now. I am seated (positionally) in the heavenlies with Jesus Christ, and I want to know what He wants me to know. I want to experience the resurrected life. I do not want to go back to the grave clothes."

CHAPTER THREE

Through Grace I Will Reckon Myself Dead unto Sin

If I am under grace, I will reckon myself dead unto sin. The Bible says in Romans 6:2 and 11, *"God forbid. How shall we, that are dead to sin, live any longer therein? Likewise* **reckon ye also yourselves to be dead indeed unto sin,** *but alive unto God through Jesus Christ our Lord."* Notice the words "reckon yourselves." The word *"reckon"* means to account, to estimate, to impute to God's account. It means to get up daily and say, "I am crucified with Christ. I am reckoning myself dead indeed unto sin. I am recognizing what happened at Calvary. Lord Jesus, as I reckon myself dead unto sin, I ask You to let me be alive to Your will for my life today. Help me, God, to be alive to You because of Your graciousness in saving me. I don't want to live for self anymore. I want to live for You today, Lord." Reckon yourself dead to sin.

If we are focused on being alive to self over Jesus Christ, then we are missing the purpose of grace. The purpose of grace is that I will reckon myself dead to sin and alive to Jesus Christ. In doing this I may grow into His likeness. *"For whom he did foreknow, he also did predestinate to be conformed to the image of his Son, that he might be the firstborn among many brethren"* (Romans 8:29).

Reckoning ourselves dead to sin involves establishing what is right and wrong. If I am going to reckon myself dead indeed to sin, I had better know what sin is. Herein lies the great controversy, the great difference between many pastors and churches today. Should a pastor, a school, or a college set some guidelines for something that may be sinful? The "radical grace" teaching is, "Heavens no! Why, that would be a 'list.'" The "radical grace" teaching is that people should reckon themselves dead unto sin, but we do not need to suggest anything that might be sinful.

God is giving you direction through His Word primarily, but also through God-given realms of authority in your life, and you and I need to give some credence to it. Does a parent have the right to make a list of what his child can listen to or watch or where he can go? I say "yes" to that. Several years ago my wife and I gave our oldest daughter ten guidelines for her relationships with boys. After reading them she said, "Thanks for the rules, Dad." Why? Because she is growing in grace. She is applying the truth of Romans 6 to her life!

I think churches should raise a standard. We need to say, "Folks, if we are going to reckon ourselves dead indeed unto sin we need to know what sin is!"

Pastors are being challenged over whether the church should prohibit young people from bringing boom boxes to camp. They are asked, "Where's that in the Bible?" We believe that if a youth pastor thinks it is a good idea to leave them at home, we are going to support him. But we live in the day of "question authority." We live in a day when the world has become so infiltrated with this idea that, under the "radical grace" doctrine, it is being advocated within the Christian life.

By the way, even the "radical grace" churches have standards. They may be different from ours. For example, we do not have preachers in our pulpit who wear their hair over their ears. But some of these who would make fun of that "standard" might not let someone serve on their church staff with a ponytail. It is not that they do not have leadership requirements; it is just that they have *different* leadership requirements.

Pastors call and write about this issue. One pastor called me and said, "Brother Chappell, pray with us. I'm not sure, but I think the best thing may be just to bring my family to your church. At the Christian school and in our area, my kids are made fun of every day for the way they dress. Something hurtful is said to them every day. My wife and I don't want them to get bitter at the ministry. Would you pray with us about my family coming to your church sometime?" I do not know if he will. But oftentimes those who supposedly "feel so guilty and shamed" by the presence of standards, are turning right around and shaming people who are trying to live for God as the Lord leads them.

We face questions like this, "Should a dress standard be allowed in a Christian school?" We say "yes," yet vast numbers of Christian parents are fighting it tooth and nail.

"Should the choir have guidelines for dress?" Lockheed Aircraft Company has guidelines for dress, but people want to argue the point for serving at the church.

We face other questions like, "Should a Christian college allow pictures of rock stars on the wall in the dorm?" People are challenging that. These are real things happening right now. I could name for you some colleges that *are* allowing pictures of rock stars on the wall in the dorm. Now someone says, "Wait, if you put that in the rule book, it is legalism." No, it is leadership stating some guidelines to help people reach spiritual maturity.

I'll quote from Dr. Pickering's book:

> Do restrictions rob us of joy? We are told that man-made rules and restrictions, passed off as biblical, become "joy-killers." Those who defend standards of living, which they believe to be based upon scriptural principles are guilty of "petty concerns and critical suspicions." They are called "stern, rigid, and cold-hearted." They are proponents of a "legalistic style of strong-arm teaching."[3]

The idea is that if there is an established rule that you cannot bring a boom box to camp, then the youth pastor is a squint-eyed legalist looking for a boom box.

Dr. Pickering goes on:

> Romans chapter six is cited as definitive in the discussion. [The popular author to which we previously referred] continually mentions the fact that those who have "lists" of "rules" are in "bondage" and must be freed. Paul, in Romans six, [this popular author] says, presents a glorious doctrine of freedom and declares that the believers are emancipated from all human "rules." Is this, however, the main thrust of Romans six?[4]

Is that what Romans 6 is all about, emancipation from human rule? I think not. I think it is all about living a holy and godly life for Jesus Christ. It's interesting that people think, if you set rules for yourself, they are okay. You set them for your family, they are okay. But let a pastor set some, and he is an ogre or joy killer.

Dr. Pickering continues:

> In this passage Paul is not dealing with "rules" but with "sin." We are not to yield to the desires of the flesh simply because we are now living under grace and not under law. Through Christ's death we have been given the power to live victoriously over the constant tug of our old nature. Since we died to our old sin nature in Christ, we are to "reckon" (count upon, accept by faith) ourselves to be "dead indeed unto sin."
>
> It is apparent by a study of the passage that Paul is not teaching that believers are free from all restrictions upon their lives. The very fact that we are dead unto sin means that there are some things we ought not to do.
>
> Our members (parts of our body) are to be yielded to God as instruments of righteousness. Righteousness is an inhibiting word, a narrowing word, a restrictive word. While Paul teaches us that we are freed from the power of sin, he also reminds us that we are the servants (slaves) to righteousness. As Christ's slaves we are restricted by the wishes of our Master. We are called slaves to God in verse 22 and as such are to aim toward holiness.[5]

The job of the pastor is to say, "Master, Lord, as we establish a church or a Christian school or a Christian college, give wisdom that we might establish this in the way You want it established because You are the head of this church, and we want this church to please You."

Dr. Pickering says:

> It is this element of "holiness" which is conspicuously absent in the work of [the popular author to which we previously referred]. Holiness is (or should be) the outgrowth of grace. The impression is received by a perusal of [this popular author's] writings that grace is an exciting liberation from all (or most) restrictions that have normally been associated with the practice of the Christian faith. If, however, we are to have our "fruit unto holiness," as Paul commands, we will be liberated from the power of sin, but restricted to the requirements for holiness. Practical holiness of life involves separation from evil.[6]

Holiness means that there are some things a believer cannot do. Godly pastors and churches through the centuries have tried earnestly, though not perfectly, to warn believers of some things that they cannot do if they would be holy. To say that such warnings are a violation of the principle of grace living is unwarranted by Scripture.

First of all, we have seen that if I live under grace, I know who I am in Christ. My flesh was crucified upon the Cross, and I have been resurrected to a new life by His grace. I do not want to look for a reason to go back to the grave clothes. I want to live the heavenly life of Jesus Christ.

Second, not only do I know who I am in Christ, but I will reckon myself dead unto sin. If you are going to reckon yourself dead unto sin, you are going to have to determine some things that are sinful. No, you won't agree with your pastor on everything on your list. You might have some things on your list that I don't have on my list, and that is real liberty. However, when we start minimizing lists of sins, we might as well throw away holiness in the Christian life. We might as well make a mockery of the commandment of God to *"Be ye holy; for I am holy"* (1 Peter 1:16b).

I realize there may be a preference I have in the way I live which someone else may not choose. But we cannot refuse scriptural truth and call it true "grace living."

CHAPTER FOUR

Through Grace I Will Yield Myself to God

If I am under grace, I will yield myself to God. Romans 6:13 says, *"Neither yield ye your members as instruments of unrighteousness unto sin: but yield yourselves unto God, as those that are alive from the dead, and your members as instruments of righteousness unto God."*

Five times in this chapter you will find the word "yield." Yield means complete surrender. It is based on the work that Christ has done. Based upon what Christ has done for me, I should say, "Lord, I want to completely surrender my life to You. You have saved me by Your grace, Lord. Help me to surrender my will to You." We should not say, "You have saved me by Your grace. Now because of Your grace let me have my will."

Let me illustrate. I refrain from watching wicked movies, not because of the law or because of some legalistic tendencies, but because of grace. Under grace and under this understanding of Christ and who I am in Christ, I am compelled to abstain from anything that would grieve Him. Because I am so thankful for what He has done for me, I do not want to grieve my Lord. I am disciplined by grace; I am under His grace. No, I am not under the law; but because I am under grace, I want to go to a higher level of holy living.

Another illustration is tithing. I tithe, but not because I am under the law. In fact, under grace many Christians far surpass the tithe year after year. Why? Because Christians who have been saved any length of time would say, "Well, under grace you should do more than what you would do under the law." If God's grace is working in your heart, creating a disposition by the Holy Spirit that makes you want to do more than what the law says, why wouldn't it be true in the matter of sanctification and holiness? No, we ought not do what we do merely because of the law, but because of a heart of grace. We should be glad to live a life that is pleasing unto Jesus Christ.

True grace is not against the law. Christ has fulfilled the law, and He gives us liberty and motivation to obey Him in Spirit and in truth.

For example, a pastor and author stated in 1991 that obedience and submission are two words that are often used in abusive churches. Last year the executive pastor of his church was interviewed by *Leadership* magazine. The church, at the time, was involved in a sixteen million dollar building program, which included a thirteen million dollar bond issue. The magazine asked about the area of tithing. Keep in mind that tithing is something that was taught as optional by this particular ministry in the early 1990s.

In his interview he stated:

Our senior pastor has confessed openly, that at [this pastor's church] in the past we have unintentionally denigrated giving. We gave people permission not to give and we were wrong. That was a hard confession.

The message of "radical grace", which we teach, for years focused on the first half of the epistle. We are freed by grace. But in a way that allowed people to ignore their obligations brought out on the last half. It wasn't said this way, but the message was clear; your behavior, your choices, your attitudes don't matter.

A real turning point for us was when we preached a sermon called, "The Spirit of the Tithe." For the first time, our church heard about tithing in a positive way. We heard that obedience is freedom.[7]

I would totally concur with this pastor's assessment of the fact that obedience is freedom. This is all we have tried to teach for years here at Lancaster Baptist Church. Titus 2:11–13 says, *"For the grace of God that bringeth salvation hath appeared to all men, Teaching us that, denying ungodliness and worldly lusts, we should live soberly, righteously, and godly, in this present world; Looking for that blessed hope, and the glorious appearing of the great God and our Saviour Jesus Christ."* We believe the grace of God teaches us to deny ungodliness and worldly lusts. We believe the grace of God does not bring freedom to not tithe or freedom to not serve God, but freedom to obey God. Now, how we obey God and how some other church obeys God, again, is a matter of individual soul liberty.

Being saved by grace does not give us an excuse to sin but a reason to obey. The Bible says that we are to yield ourselves to God, and whatever we yield ourselves to will become our master. Romans 6:16 says, *"Know ye not, that to whom ye yield yourselves servants to obey, his servants ye are to whom ye obey; whether of sin unto death, or of obedience unto righteousness?"* So we must yield ourselves to God and let Him be our Master. That is all under His grace.

The function of grace is not only to liberate us from the power of sin, but to make us servants to Jesus Christ. To some that is an oxymoron, but that is a theological principle we need to understand. If you think that as a servant to Christ you can frequent night clubs, then you have a different concept of grace! I can still love you and you can still be my brother or sister in Christ, but you are not going to teach fifth-grade girls at Lancaster Baptist Church and tell them about it.

Grace is why an apostle such as James said, *"James, a servant of God and of the Lord Jesus Christ...."* Because you had to, James? Because the apostles made a list, and they put you on it, and you are in bondage, and that is why you are a servant? No! Because of God's grace I gladly am a servant to Jesus Christ. What a high principle of living!

I would urge you to define, from the Bible, this matter of God's grace. Understand that we simply believe grace is a study in Christian conduct that brings me closer to God and to His will, not further away and into my own self will.

Regarding the discipline of grace, Dr. Pickering writes:

> The impression given by [this popular author] is that the sole function of grace is to liberate. He celebrates continually the believer's freedom,

liberation, and deliverance from restrictions either real or imagined. Grace gives us permission to be free (he says). We have liberating grace. All who embrace grace become free indeed. You will be free. You should be enjoying your liberty. These are but a few examples; many more could be listed.

Our brother, in authoring his book, seems to be obsessed with the great bondage under which the believers seem to labor. After reading his writings this author could not help but ask himself, "Why have you never felt this great burden of bondage about which he writes?" I was raised in a very strict holiness home. I attended a Christian college that would be viewed as having very restrictive rules. I have ministered in, and been pastor of churches that maintained high standards of conduct for their members and leaders. In the years of my ministry I have never felt that I was in bondage to any human nor misused. I have never felt restive under rules or restrictions. It is interesting that in recent years this seems to have become a problem for some. Why? I believe it is because of the tremendous pressure of the wicked age in which we live. Holy, godly, and separated living is no longer in style. It is viewed as an anachronism and a bother. God's grace is being used by some as a way by which to allow Christians to do things they have not done before with the idea that it is perfectly acceptable. Some Christian leaders and their followers are caving in to the spirit of the age.[8]

While it is certainly true that grace liberates us, it is equally true that grace calls us to serve. The New Testament is not only about what we *can* do, but it is also about what we *cannot* do. This is the aspect of grace that is being neglected today. We certainly do not intend to "major on the minors" in our ministry. Our goal is to lift up Christ. Yet, I do not want to minimize the fact that Christ is worthy of my best—He wants my life to be totally consecrated unto Him!

CHAPTER FIVE

The Biblical Approach to Grace

You say, "Well, if we understand God's grace properly, how will we approach the ministry?" We will approach ministry as the servants of Christ who are grateful for what He has done, and we will serve Him from grateful and thankful hearts.

I am convinced that we must not only celebrate the liberation of grace, but we must also understand the purification of grace. I thank God for the liberation of grace. His grace has set me free. John 8:32 says, *"And ye shall know the truth, and the truth shall make you free."* But I am not free to do what *I* want to do. I am free to obey Christ now.

A false idea of freedom is ruining America. There are people in Hollywood who believe that they have the freedom of speech to portray wicked things on the side of buildings under the guise of their freedom as Americans. They are ruining their lives in the process. Even so, I believe Christians are ruining their lives with the "radical grace" movement.

Titus 2:11–13 says, *"For the grace of God that bringeth salvation hath appeared to all men, Teaching us that, denying ungodliness and worldly lusts, we should live soberly, righteously, and godly, in this present world; Looking for that blessed hope, and the glorious appearing of the great God and our Saviour Jesus Christ."* That is what grace teaches me to do. I believe I can honestly say that I endeavor to communicate love to people from different churches when they ask about differences. I want to establish that we love people no matter what differing opinions they have. But I honestly feel sorry for Christians who determine to loose themselves from the supposed bondage or control of godly landmarks in their lives. They will find that their newfound freedom will lead them only to further bondage, and then they will have too much pride to admit they stepped out of line in the first place.

How about the prodigal son? He said, "Hey, Dad, I don't want all this mess here. I want my freedom!" He went on his own way and, yes, he had his freedom. But that freedom ruined his life.

People who think that finding their own liberty and writing their own ticket is the way to happiness do not find happiness. However, serving Jesus Christ will always bring happiness.

It is not a theological contradiction. You and I need to realize it is a command. Romans 6 states that I am to yield my members as instruments, not of unrighteousness unto sin but unto God. It is possible then to live under grace and still have in our lives and church some standards of conduct by which we will live.

Romans 14:7 gives us a final compelling thought regarding these issues, *"For none of us liveth to himself, and no man dieth to himself."* As society decays and as churches acquiesce, one reason we must be very strong is that there are some children coming behind us. For every step down we take in these matters, our children are going to take several steps more. I am convinced that you will attend many Christian churches twenty or thirty years from now that will not remotely resemble "church."

Recently, my wife was wallpapering a bathroom at home. I noticed she had started about a few inches from the corner. I asked her why she didn't line the wallpaper up at the corner. She said the corner was slightly crooked, and that if she lined up on the corner, the wallpaper would be a foot or two off by the time she got around the room. Consequently, she made a straight line (a plumb line) on the wall and started there. Friends, I have seen families change just a little bit. I have seen pastors drop their stand slightly. Ten years later, you hardly recognize the family or the church.

God has given us a "plumb line." It is called the Bible. We need to stay true to the Bible, lest our lives, having lined up slightly wrong today, are devastated down the road.

You say, "Well, it is okay to lower our standard if we are reaching people." No, the doctrine will soon be absent from these churches. These churches are looking more like late night talk shows with few conversions.

In our church, we believe that you can live a holy life and still be living under the grace of God. But we must look, not only at our liberty, but also at our responsibility.

As we live a life under grace, we will know who we are in Christ. We will reckon ourselves dead indeed unto sin and alive unto Christ; and we will yield our instruments not as the servants of unrighteousness, but as the servants of God.

We see the old grace and the radical grace. The old grace will fill you up. The radical grace will leave you empty. Oh, you will get to do some things you used to do before you got saved, and you'll even have some people saying it is okay. But you will be empty.

I want to challenge you, as grace is being redefined, to let the grace of God cause you to become more like Jesus Christ rather than more like you were before you were saved!

CHAPTER SIX

Grace and the Christian Leader

Over the past fifteen to twenty years there has been much study, evaluation, criticism and adjustment in the leadership philosophies of Bible-believing churches. Some of this discussion has been led by men who were involved in a very strict upbringing and have apparently reacted against their past church upbringing by categorizing it as being abusive or hurtful. To counteract their bad experiences in previous churches, some of these emerging church leaders began to develop and teach a concept called "radical grace." The teaching generally says that a ministry philosophy that emphasizes faithfulness in areas such as tithing, church attendance, or witnessing is a church that is, or somehow may be, abusing people.

While these men may have identified some potential imbalances in ministry, the "radical grace" approach to solving the problem has allowed many people to simply classify good and godly environments of spiritual growth as abusive, harsh or hurtful simply because they disagree with the way said churches choose to worship and serve the Lord.

I dealt, at great length, with some of these questions in a book I wrote several years ago entitled *Guided by Grace*. Some of my observations, at that time, were as follows:

> A final and significant concern for the church and its leadership is abuse. We might think by listening to some that have been hurt in church-related ministries that another twelve-step program was needed for "recovering churchgoers." While some of the claims of abuse may be questionable, leaders must be willing to evaluate their ministry philosophy and practices in the light of Scripture. We must confirm that God's grace is both evident and working in the church. I do believe there are abusive or negative leadership styles and techniques that should be avoided if our desire is to foster an environment of servant leadership in the church.

> Godly leadership and authority are conferred by God and must not be grasped or seized. An effective spiritual leader will always lead from a position of authority, but we must keep in mind that the authority is a gift from God and not something earned for self or self-gratification. Such fleshly approaches to leadership birth a critical, self-promoting spirit in the church, born of the leader and imitated by the people. This in turn creates an environment of competition, division and dissension of which the shepherd himself is the instigator....

God's love and grace must motivate the spiritual leader. Otherwise, he will adversely affect the spiritual development of those he is called to serve. He will easily lose touch with the mind of God for the vision and pace of the ministry....

Ironically, many Christian psychologists and authors of the 1990s discovered a market among those who were hurting. Soon followed a proliferation of books and materials published on subjects related to abuse, which caused their readers to dwell upon their distrust instead of trusting in the healing and forgiveness of Christ.

A comforting and miraculous fact is that our God is the living God of the past, present, and future. He owns time. We cannot go back in time and recover or soothe our past emotional distress, but the God Who creates and keeps time can be active in our past, present, and future simultaneously, shaping us into the instrument of His choosing by using our experiences for His glory. Adversely, "Satan likes us best when we are completely absorbed in trying to figure ourselves out, because at such moments, all forward motion stops."[9] As J. Oswald Sanders once stated, "Peace is not the absence of trouble, but the presence of God."[10]

The result of the present-day climate of suspicion has been both positive and negative. Positively, Christian ministries and spiritual leaders are taking regular spiritual inventory of their motives and mode of ministry....

...we have acknowledged that some in spiritual leadership have caused hurt, confusion, and suspicion by their actions. Yet, sadly, many leaders today are also being hurt and maligned by those whom they have tried to serve. Many of those Christians who speak woefully against those in leadership claim they must do so because they would only be ridiculed or ignored if they went directly to a church leader; but this is often a smokescreen, for in reality most leaders would welcome an opportunity for a godly meeting in an effort to glorify Christ. Those in the reactionary paradigm seem to take pleasure in and feed on their self-appointed position of blame-thrower. However, God is not as interested in assigning blame as He is in resolving problems. His desire is reconciliation.

Spiritual leaders are not perfect people. They must be allowed to grow, and they should be willing to accept godly admonitions; but the angry and suspicious rarely allow for this growth; and while they talk of prayer and grace, their actions tend to be harsh and legalistic toward the leader. In fact, the very judgments and abuses they claim to have experienced are ammunition in their exploits to war against the authority of their spiritual leaders.

Detractors will always challenge the vision of leadership. We hear it in phrases like: "That little congregation will never accomplish that"; "They're just interested in numbers"; or "The pastor is on an ego trip." The leader must rise above such criticism. He must stand tall on his knees if he is to see above the crowd....

Those who have been discouraged by a leader or mentor are wise to give the matter to the Lord, Who will judge in righteous judgment.

Also, it is wise to remember that spiritual leaders will grow in grace over time. For example, I recently met a friend whom I remembered as a seventh grade school yard playmate. He was rough and not very bright in school, as I recall. Today, twenty-five years later, he is a successful businessman. Similarly, someone you remember as harsh may have grown in grace and continued in Christian service.

Sometimes it is not the messenger that is despised or suspected as much as it is the message he preaches. Dr. John R. Rice advised: "It is no strange thing that modern evangelists—that is, honest, Bible-preaching, Spirit-filled evangelists— these days are criticized and hated and abused. So it has always been with men of God who paid the price for revival! When men slandered Moody and called him 'Crazy Moody,' when men mocked at Billy Sunday's preaching and accused him of preaching for money, it was no more than should be expected by anyone who would follow in the steps of Elijah, seeking to prevail with God for revival."[11] The Apostle Paul understood this price when he exhorted Timothy to "*endure hardness, as a good soldier of Jesus Christ*" (2 Timothy 2:3).

The ridicule and abuse that leaders experience is not limited to a particular denomination. It is not limited to a particular leadership style. Wherever leaders lead biblically, adversity will be present and abuse of the leader may follow.

Growing Ministries Face Adversity

In my next comments, **I do not wish to endorse the ministry philosophy of any particular**

leader; however, I think it interesting to note the common denominators of their experience. I have included comments about or by men from various backgrounds because each of them has been on the receiving end of statements intended to hurt or hinder his ministry.

The following statements were printed about Jerry Falwell, a pastor in Virginia, in *Christianity Today*, December 9, 1996: "...some **former supporters** say [he] has achieved his goals through a stifling authoritarianism, and that his organization's growth has been inhibited by his overly controlling methods."[12] Did you notice the quote was from "former supporters"? This man is certainly not perfect, but he does have thousands of former and present supporters and employees who appreciate his leadership and contributions. **Every ministry** in America—whether Baptist, Presbyterian, Pentecostal, etc.—has some former supporters who would now disagree with that ministry....

Later in the same article the author states, "...[This pastor] has convinced his followers that his word carries a special measure of authority."[13] Again the author of this ecumenical magazine article characterizes this man as a spiritual criminal who has convinced people of something that any leader could be accused of.

Another pastor in Texas provides an additional example. This man passed the mantle of his ministry to a "Timothy" after fifty years of serving as pastor. However, this "Timothy" proved both unfaithful and critical when he resigned his new post and disseminated a scathing report of his mentor's leadership. This depiction included words and phrases like "deceit" and "den of treachery." He even referred to his one-time mentor, W.A. Criswell, now 84, as a conning, power-hungry tyrant.

While there may be those who aspire to leadership for the wrong reasons, this author highly doubts that this senior pastor faithfully preached and served for fifty years because of a lust for power or due to selfish motives. Most men who become pastors of mega-churches have succeeded in the ministry because they inspire those around them to work in concert. The commitment necessary for such a task excludes a hunger for power and greed as legitimate motivations.

This retired pastor's fifty-year ministry must have been motivated by a love for Jesus. His critic has since divorced and remarried since his resignation and has shared that if he returns to the pulpit, it will be in a small church.

Again we see a man who was helped and mentored disagreeing and reacting in a less-than-graceful way. What was the result? The secular media reported of their difference, and the Devil sat in the corner laughing. Although the senior pastor resumed his preaching ministry, we have no doubt that he was grieved by this situation.

Another pastor in Phoenix, Arizona, Tommy Barnett, of First Assembly of God, experienced incredible scrutiny and hurtful innuendo during a building program. He reveals in his book, "We became the talk of the town with a few even suggesting I was some wild cult leader with Jim Jones-like persuasion and a pocketful of money gleaned from foolish and duped attendees...it seemed everyone wanted to go public with their comments, whether they were based on facts or not."[14] This is one more example of a dynamic leader, serving to the best of his ability, being questioned and abused in his own community. Those who supported their pastor were referred to as being "duped," and a common term appointed to those who appreciate the leadership models in their churches.

Again, Charles Stanley, a pastor in Atlanta, reports in his book that some people in his church seemed concentrated on defaming him during a difficult time in his ministry. He remembers that "the next Wednesday night, which was a business meeting, I asked the church to give my Sunday school superintendent and me the full authority to appoint all the deacons and church officers. A member of the original opposition stood and gave a speech about how we were running him out of the church, and then he said, 'If you don't watch what you're doing, you're going to get hurt.' With that he hit me with the back of his hand in the face."[15] Perhaps this pastor's philosophy was not pleasing to a small group in the church, but the resulting defamation of character and physical assault by those who were suspicious of his intent were certainly not pleasing to Christ.

With these few examples in mind, we see a pattern developing that teaches us that spiritual leaders will be the recipients of the very tactics the suspicious or hurting claim they have received....

Those who hold a spiritual leader in suspicion will ultimately doubt everything about the leader's life and ministry. As a result of this suspicion, a re-labeling of ministry terms usually occurs:

Legitimate Terms	Re-labeled Terms
preaching/teaching	bashing/shaming
decisive biblical leadership	authoritarianism
local church	a system/organized religion
vision/direction	an agenda
soulwinning/evangelism	recruiting
care group leaders/deacons	informants

While shameful pulpits where people are named and ridiculed do exist, another tragedy is developing. Specifically, cynically-minded parishioners view all preaching as bashing, all strong leadership as authoritarian. The challenge is found in the fact that leadership that is not strong is not leadership at all. Often those who could justly benefit by the leadership of a parent or pastor never experience this benefit because of their false perceptions or personal rejection of spiritual leadership. Many in our society and in our Christian culture today reject the absolute nature of the Christian faith. Many desire spiritual experiences, choices, preferences, and comfort instead of knowledge, absolutes, truth, and growth. Such people prefer to make up their own way and their own faith instead of following the One Who is the Way, the Truth and the Life.

Additionally, it is wrong to label a ministry that preaches the pure Gospel of grace as a "system" or "organized religion" that is merely following human agendas. These hurtful labels are carelessly thrown like grenades without regard for the church leader who happens to be in the path of the tiny weapon with the big blast.

Every ministry will reflect some of the weak human characteristics of its leadership and membership. In fact, there will never be a perfect church on this earth as long as there are people in it. Therefore, as believers and leaders we must determine to follow the counsel of God's Word to grow in the grace and knowledge of our Lord Jesus Christ....

If a leader has been too harsh in his style, he must ask God to change his disposition. In deed, he may never satisfy everybody, but that is not the goal. The goal is to follow Jesus and to edify His people.

To avoid confusion, consider the difference between pleasing the congregation and edifying the congregation. **To please** people, is to make them happy or satisfied, fulfill their wishes and wills. **To edify** is to instruct so as to promote intellectual and moral improvement.

Suspicious, skeptical, and, yes, hurting persons can react against leadership to the point that they begin to lose balance in and perspective on the Christian life. The suspicious and cynical person will reject nearly anything the parent, pastor, or leader teaches him. Often a good principle is rejected merely because someone else used to say that. The person who has become cynical becomes the very thing he accused. The Bible states in Proverbs 11:1 that *"a false balance is abomination."*[16]

To be honest, after *Guided by Grace* was published, I was actually criticized by some conservative, Christian leaders for emphasizing the necessity of growing in grace and modeling a servant style of leadership. In reality, we have at times in our ministry, experienced comments from those who feel we are too conservative or "harsh" in our approach to leadership, and others who feel that we are too soft and do not have strong enough "standards."

To help with developing a proper ministry philosophy, I have tried to walk on the following pathway of leadership development…

Remember, the Church Is the Lord's

Firstly, I have tried to remember daily, that the church is the Lord's. Acts 20:28 says, *"Take heed therefore unto yourselves, and to all the flock, over the which the Holy Ghost hath made you overseers, to feed the church of God, which he hath purchased with his own blood."*

Yes, the Lord has placed me here to be an overseer, but I have constantly remembered that I am the under shepherd and Jesus Christ is the Chief Shepherd. He owns the church and will bring each of us into account one day.

Remain Teachable

Secondly, I have tried not to ignore even critical comments over the years that have been made toward me and our ministry. I have asked the Holy Spirit to help me walk in such a way that I would consider and make adjustments. I can honestly say that our church is probably a more balanced, gentle, and loving church today because we have grown in God's grace. We have, however, endeavored to maintain our distinctiveness as a Baptist church that chooses to worship God in grace and truth.

Remain Accountable

Thirdly, I have tried to remain accountable as a pastor, firstly and foremost to the Lord, and secondly, to godly men who have helped me in shaping and developing our ministry philosophy. Dr. David Gibbs, Jr., Dr. Don Sisk, and Dr. R.B. Ouellette are men with whom I regularly meet, for the purpose of spiritual growth, fellowship, and assessment. Several other men of God have been kind and helpful to me in this way. We discuss my spirit toward the Lord, my family, this ministry, and the ministry in general. When I am going through a season of trial or criticism, I share with them the e-mails, letters, or comments that are made, in their entirety.

Work with the Deacons

On a local level, I have endeavored to be very transparent with the twenty-nine deacons of our church. The Scriptures do not command a pastor to "submit" to the deacons in the sense of church government, but on the other hand I believe we are all to be spiritually accountable, one to another, and I gladly share, with our deacons, various personal and spiritual prayer requests. I also endeavor to foster an environment with them that often brings questions and comments that are very helpful to me. The deacons are well aware of church finances, and they know the status of my personal finances and giving as well.

In short, as a pastor and pastoral leadership team at Lancaster Baptist Church, we are doing the best we know to do, using the Word of God as our guide and seeking the filling of the Holy Spirit on a daily basis. We also want to be spiritual enough to be willing to change and to adjust, to constantly seek a proper balance in the ministry. We have not yet arrived, nor will we, until we see the Lord Jesus.

Love People

There are thousands of happy, growing people who are ministered to at Lancaster Baptist Church. Hundreds of them have elements in their lifestyles with which I personally, as a Christian leader, disagree, yet they are loved. Scores of marriages are strengthened through our ministry. The people who attend here are not blinded or ignorantly duped and deceived into participating in worship with us.

Develop Hearts for God

As we continue developing as spiritual leaders, we will keep our emphasis as it is clearly stated in our church purpose statement: **To develop people with a heart for God.** Our emphasis has been on preaching, teaching, and encouraging people to cultivate their heart walk with the Lord. How their change of heart is reflected in an outward manifestation is something between them and God. Meanwhile, we will continue fostering an environment that is conducive to grace and growth. We will continue promoting and believing that acceptance is the optimum environment for growth and will accept people where they are and allow them to grow at their own pace. We will not, however, apologize for having certain requirements for church leaders that we believe are based in the Scriptures.

On the other hand, there are churches that start off in the "radical grace" mode and have also had to make some shifts back toward the realm of Scriptural obedience in order to maintain balance in their lives and ministries. I gave an example of a ministry like this in chapter four.

The pastors who stated that their message in the early 1990s was: "your behavior, your choices, your attitudes don't matter" found a ready audience. This message is one on which people again are seizing. People who are members of conservative, fervent churches, who no longer desire to have the same level of commitment as the church they are currently attending, find empowerment and justification by the radical grace concepts and the church abuse statements.

Our point in this matter of church philosophy is simply this: If someone feels he would rather worship in a different style, with a different level of commitment— time scheduling, or whatever—he should simply find the place that best suits him and lovingly and kindly begin serving there.

Again, every Christian is on a spiritual journey. Christians who are harsh, legalistic, or judgmental need to grow in grace to the point that they would not even resemble abusive ministry. On the other hand, Christians who are so involved in "radical grace" that they begin to have choices, behavior, and attitudes that are unbecoming of the Scripture, need to come back to the reality that "obedience is freedom."

PART TWO

Christian Liberty

CHAPTER SEVEN

Redefining Words

Stand fast therefore in the liberty wherewith Christ hath made us free, and be not entangled again with the yoke of bondage.—Galatians 5:1

For, brethren, ye have been called unto liberty; only use not liberty for an occasion to the flesh, but by love serve one another.—Galatians 5:13

Has it ever occurred to you that over the years the meaning of a word can change? I can remember when the word "gay" meant happy. Yet, today when somebody uses the word "gay" it is in reference to a sinful, wicked lifestyle that is against God and His Word. It is the same word, yet twenty-five to thirty years later it has a completely different meaning.

Another word that has changed is "conservative." I believe that we are seeing a redefinition of this word. Five or ten years ago, if someone was called conservative in this country, it meant that he probably had some Judeo-Christian ethics. It meant that he was probably against the murder of unborn babies and other sinful practices in society. Now we are coming to the point that the word "conservative" is more of an economic term.

I also think of the word "Baptist." Thirty or forty years ago, when someone said, "I am a member of a Baptist church," there were certain given understandings that would come to mind. Being a Baptist usually meant that you attended church Sunday morning, Sunday night, and Wednesday night. This was a given about Baptists. Baptists have always been that kind of people. We have practiced the assembling of ourselves together.

Baptists have always had certain dogma. For example, the inerrancy of the Scriptures was always something you could just bank on with the Baptists. There was also a certain standard of separation for which the Baptists were known. Historically, for example, Baptists stood against the sale and consumption of liquor. Most Baptist churches had a covenant that stated this conviction. That was just something the Baptists did.

Perhaps you have used the word "Baptist" and someone has said, "Oh, you mean the hell-fire, damnation ones?" That is the way some people view Baptists. Today, there is a whole new trend in Baptist churches to be less offensive. The word "Baptist" is being redefined. What "Baptist" used to mean is quite different than what it generally means today.

Below is a church covenant from a Southern Baptist church in 1954. Southern Baptists have a rich heritage, just like our country, yet many things have changed over the years. In 1954, this is what every member of the church signed and promised:

> Having been led, as we believe by the Spirit of God to receive the Lord Jesus as our Saviour and, on the profession of our faith, having been baptized in the name of the Father, the Son, and the Holy Spirit, we do now in the presence of God and this assembly most solemnly and joyfully enter into the covenant with one another as one body in Christ.
>
> We engage, therefore, by the Holy Spirit to walk together in Christian love; to strive for the advancement of the church in knowledge, holiness, and comfort; to promote its prosperity and spirituality; to sustain its worship, ordinances, discipline, doctrines; to contribute cheerfully and regularly to the support of this ministry, the expenses of the church, the relief of the poor, and to spread the Gospel through all nations.
>
> We also engage to maintain family devotions; to religiously educate our children; to seek the salvation of our kindred and acquaintances; to walk circumspectly in the world; to be just in our dealings, faithful in our engagements, exemplary in our deportment; to avoid all tattling, backbiting, excessive anger; to abstain from the sale and use of intoxicating drinks as a beverage; to be zealous in reference; to advance the kingdom of our Saviour.
>
> We further engage to watch over each other in brotherly love; to remember one another in prayer; to aid one another in sickness and distress; to cultivate Christian sympathy and feelings of Christian courtesy in speech; to be slow to take offense, but always ready for reconciliation and

mindful of the rules of our Saviour to secure without delay.

We moreover engage that when we remove from this place we will, as soon as possible, unite with some other church where we can carry out the spirit of this covenant and principles of God's Word.

That was what Baptists believed in 1954. They believed certain doctrines. They believed it so much that they signed it. You would be hard pressed to get some Southern Baptists to sign that today; or if they signed it, you would be hard pressed to get them to live it.

Below is an article from a denominational Baptist paper in 1954:

Certainly Baptist people should stand against habitually worshipping with mixed groups of other denominations. It is our God-given right to worship as we choose, but as Baptists, and according to the teachings of God's Word, we should separate ourselves and be of one mind and one body.

This is from a denomination that no longer believes this, and they now support the World Council of Churches. Their definition of the word "Baptist" has changed over the years.

Years ago, the word "Baptist" immediately brought certain things to mind: certain doctrines, certain dogma, and certain positions. Now when you mention a Baptist church you have to do much research to find out if it is a Baptist church or a Baptist-in-name-only church.

So words, over the years, have a way of changing. The word "gay" has changed; the word "conservative" is being redefined; and the word "Baptist" has definitely been redefined.

I think of the word "Christian." *"...And the disciples were called Christians first in Antioch"* (Acts 11:26). Years ago, when someone was a Christian, immediately people would think, "Oh, he is a Christian. He is a Christ follower, a Christ-like one. He is not going to do certain things, or she's not going to look a certain way." This is how Christians used to be. When you say that someone is a Christian now, most people have a different understanding of the word. It used to mean "Christ-like-one." People would assume that if you were a "Christ-like-one" you would not do anything that Jesus would not do.

For example, we have Christian bookstores today that sell rock music. "Well, it is Christian rock," they say. That is like Christian immorality! I do not think you can put those two together. You see the word "Christian" is different now than it used to be.

Another word I think of as being redefined is "liberty." Liberty meant, in days past, freedom to be responsible. There was a liberty to obey the law. As an American, I am free to obey the law. Liberty today means to some people that they can burn our U.S. flag. To some it means that they can sing rap music songs about killing women and police officers as well as raping women. The meaning of the word "liberty" has changed.

In Christianity, many of God's people have misunderstood and even redefined the subject of Christian liberty. The word "liberty," for some Christians, is a code word for a rebellious heart. A catch phrase that Christians use is, "Well, I have liberty." What they mean is that they have a rebellious heart, and they think that liberty is a Bible word that can justify sin.

In my life, I believe in and practice Christian liberty. I am alive to Christ and His grace, but I do not practice Christian liberty at the disposal of my Christian testimony or at the disposal of my Christian responsibility. Christian liberty should never be carried out at the expense of a Christian testimony. In the following chapters, I want to share with you some biblical insight concerning Christian liberty. We will see the biblical meaning of the word "liberty," how it has been redefined, and how we can refocus our lives based upon a clear understanding of our liberty in Christ.

CHAPTER EIGHT

The Meaning of Christian Liberty

Stand fast therefore in the liberty wherewith Christ hath made us free, and be not entangled again with the yoke of bondage.—Galatians 5:1

The word "liberty" means freedom from bondage. To fully understand the context of this passage, we must continue reading. *"Behold, I Paul say unto you, that if ye be circumcised, Christ shall profit you nothing"* (Galatians 5:2). This very verse should be a signal to you that we are now reading about the Mosaic Law. *"For I testify again to every man that is circumcised, that he is a debtor to do the whole law. Christ is become of no effect unto you, whosoever of you are justified by the law; ye are fallen from grace. For we through the Spirit wait for the hope of righteousness by faith. For in Jesus Christ neither circumcision availeth any thing, nor uncircumcision; but faith which worketh by love"* (Galatians 5:3–6). In verse 4, "fallen from grace" does not mean that these Christians were losing their salvation. It means that they were simply making salvation of no effect in their daily lives. Notice in verse 7 he says, *"Ye did run well; who did hinder you that ye should not obey the truth?"*

We are reading here of people who were set free from the bondage of the Mosaic Law. They were off and running in the Christian life; then, according to the context in the book of Galatians, some of the Judaizers (those who trusted in the Mosaic Law for justification) were grabbing hold of these Christians and pulling them back. Many times a Christian can be put back into the bondage of a false religious system, as was true in this case. These new Christians were running freely, but then they again became trapped by the bondage of the law. The legalists (those who were grabbing hold of the new Christians) were adding something to salvation other than God's grace as a free gift. The term "legalist" simply refers to those who add works to salvation. Someone who says you have to do some work to get saved is a legalist because they are adding a law to salvation that God did not add. So the word "liberty" meant that Christians were free from the bondage of a false religious system.

Freedom from bondage is what is meant in Galatians 5:1 when Paul says, *"Stand fast therefore in the liberty wherewith Christ hath made us free...."* Paul was telling the Galatians, who were being plagued by the Judaizers, to stand fast in the doctrines of Jesus Christ and not to get tangled up again in teachings that would drag them away from freedom in Jesus Christ. In the context, liberty is not really referring to some of the areas that Christians bring up today. It is actually speaking of the doctrinal liberty and then the positional liberty that we have in Jesus Christ by being freed from sin.

When I got saved, I sensed extreme liberty in my life. I felt like I was set free. Isaiah 61:1 says, *"The Spirit of the Lord GOD is upon me; because the LORD hath anointed me to preach good tidings unto the meek; he hath sent me to bind up the brokenhearted, to proclaim liberty to the captives, and the opening of the prison to them that are bound."* When someone is saved, Jesus Christ comes into his life. His sins are forgiven. He is set free from the bondage of sin. He has power in Jesus Christ to live a life that is no longer in bondage to sin. In this truth, we find the secondary meaning of Christian liberty: the forgiveness of and the setting free from sin. In Romans 8:2, Paul said, *"For the law of the Spirit of life in Christ Jesus hath made me free from the law of sin and death."* In Jesus Christ, he had freedom from sin and death. Furthermore, in 2 Corinthians 3:17, the Bible says, *"Now the Lord is that Spirit: and where the Spirit of the Lord is, there is liberty."* When you were saved and the Holy Spirit indwelt your life, there was freedom from sin, forgiveness in your heart, and liberty to serve the Lord Jesus Christ.

In 1972, when I was saved, the burden was lifted. I was free from sin and free to serve the Lord Jesus Christ. I had liberty to serve the Lord Jesus Christ based upon what He had done in my life. Liberty is freedom from the Old Testament law; it is freedom from and the forgiveness of sin.

The problem is that some Christians use "liberty" as their code word or rationale for a life that is not separated to Christ. Romans 12:1-2 says, *"I beseech you therefore, brethren, by the mercies of God, that ye present your bodies a living sacrifice, holy, acceptable unto God, which is your reasonable service. And be not conformed to this world: but be ye transformed by the renewing of your mind, that ye may prove what is that good, and acceptable, and perfect, will of God.*" "Liberty" has become the term some Christians use to justify a lifestyle that is conformed to this world's ungodly culture. Herein lies the danger of abusing and redefining Christian liberty. Liberty is simply freedom from sin and freedom to serve Christ from a genuine heart of love. It is not an excuse to live a lifestyle that quenches the Holy Spirit.

In our church there are some guidelines that we established years ago for our church leaders. For example, we have asked the ushers in the church to wear ties when they are on duty. We have also said that our ladies who teach in Sunday school must wear dresses when they are teaching. I have never said, nor will I ever say, that wearing a tie or a dress makes our leaders better Christians or makes them "more saved." Outward conformity does not create or guarantee a pure heart inwardly. Our dress requirements for leaders have nothing to do with our spiritual status. If I were to link your appearance to your heart by saying that if you appear a certain way then you have a clean heart, I would be misinterpreting the Word of God. I do believe, however, that a man's outward appearance is often a reflection of his heart. I believe that, in time, a Christian will understand that church is not where you wear your very worst. By the way, on any given Sunday we have people attend our church in jeans or tank tops, and we are always glad that they have come!

Let me shock you. I believe that somebody can attend church in cutoff jeans and a tank top and have a more pure heart than some of our cleanest dressed Christian men with suits and ties! Just because someone looks or acts a certain way does not guarantee that he has a pure heart or is a good Christian. Below is an interesting article that I found recently:

> I was a little surprised by the questions I received prior to the visit of some special guests regarding our dress code. I see many people wearing clothes that would be more appropriate for mowing the lawn on Saturday morning or picnicking at the beach or park. It is here that I introduce the word "pride." Clearly, if one must ask if he or she is appropriately dressed for a visit by a special guest, then perhaps we have gone too far in our casualness, and we have lost perspective of the appropriate time to so dress. I would suggest that professionalism goes beyond our daily business transactions and includes the manner in which we present ourselves. Appropriate dress is a measure of respect we hold for ourselves and each other in this organization. The pride we have in ourselves and in our organization should never result in wondering if our clothing is appropriate. We all take great pride in our organization; let's show it in the way we dress.[17]

You would say, "Well, Pastor, which old-fashioned, fundamental Baptist, Bible-preaching guy said that?" Jack Gordon, the President of Lockheed, said it. A rebellious person would say, "He is a legalist; what about my liberty?" In actuality, very few employees would fight Jack Gordon on this issue because he signs their paycheck. Yet, in writing this to his employees, this corporate president is not saying that if they dress a certain way they will be smarter! He is not being a legalist; he is being a leader. He is not abusing the liberty of his employees; he is doing his job!

When police officers have an inspection from a superior officer, they don't question why they have to polish the brass and shine the shoes! No police officer is going to say, "What about my liberty, man?" (At least not if he expects to stay employed.) In many areas, the leader is always considered to be "mean" or a dictator. People with a rebellious heart will always call a leader another name other than a leader. Always.

We have seen that liberty in the biblical context of Galatians 1 means that Christians are free from the yoke of bondage under the law (or system of works). They are free from the burden of sin and have liberty to do what is right.

CHAPTER NINE

The Misinterpretation of Liberty

Misinterpretation #1

"I have the liberty to sin."

Apparently, the abuse of liberty did not start with liberalism or rebellion in the 1990s. From the book of Galatians we can see that there were people misunderstanding this even in the first century. Notice what Paul says in Galatians 5:13, "*For, brethren, ye have been called unto liberty; only use not liberty for an occasion to the flesh, but by love serve one another.*" He calls the Galatians "brethren." Let me state that even if you misuse your liberty, you are still my Christian brother if you have accepted Christ as your personal Saviour. Paul was not rejecting the Galatians. He was saying, "Brethren, wait a minute, you have been called unto liberty; you are free in Jesus Christ, *only use not liberty for an occasion to the flesh.*" Paul said in Titus 2:11-12, "*For the grace of God that bringeth salvation hath appeared to all men, Teaching us that,*" *denying ungodliness and worldly lusts, we should live soberly, righteously, and godly, in this present world."*

In other words, do not say, "I have liberty now in Christ, and my sins are forgiven, so I can go back to the Mosaic Law; I can go back to my old lifestyle." Paul says, "Don't use your liberty as an occasion to the flesh, or as a license to sin." Notice also, he said that God's grace teaches us to deny an ungodly lifestyle.

A proper understanding of grace does not cause flippant living. God's grace creates a holy disposition in the life of a believer whereby he or she learns to deny worldliness. This gives greater clarity to the definition of liberty. It is freedom to serve. Notice what else he says in Galatians 5:13–15, *"For, brethren, ye have been called unto liberty; only use not liberty for an occasion to the flesh, but by love serve one another. For all the law is fulfilled in one word, even in this; Thou shalt love thy neighbour as thyself. But if ye bite and devour one another, take heed that ye be not consumed one of another."*

The first misinterpretation of liberty is that you can use liberty as an occasion to the flesh. Paul deliberately says that liberty should never be an excuse for sin. Liberty is not a license to do whatever you want to do. Liberty is not a license to gossip. It is not a license for any lady in the church to talk about another lady in a wrong way. It is not a license for any pastor to talk about another pastor in a wrong way. Galatians 5:15 deals specifically with gossip when Paul says, *"But if ye bite and devour one another, take heed that ye be not consumed one of another."* He is saying that though you are forgiven for sin, this doesn't mean you can start biting and devouring your Christian brothers like a piranha!

Somebody who has strife in his heart (one who is against another person, whether it be in the work place, in the home, or in the church) is acting "earthly, sensual and devilish." James 3:17 states, *"But the wisdom that is from above is first pure, then peaceable...."* Someone who is truly wise will be a peacemaker. He will not use his liberty to voice his differences in a hurtful way. A godly person will be a peacemaker. You cannot spread peace by spreading your wrong attitude. James continues describing godly wisdom as, *"peaceable, gentle, and easy to be intreated, full of mercy and good fruits, without partiality, and without hypocrisy."* A righteous person will not use his liberty to say whatever he wants to say or to "speak his mind." Technically, I could use my liberty to stand in the pulpit and say whatever I want to say; God would forgive me. Every pastor must pray that he will not speak "in the flesh." Yet, because I want to say only what He wants said in His pulpit, I am not going to abuse my liberty.

Furthermore, no Christian should ever speak his mind in a hurtful way simply because he has liberty or forgiveness. A righteous person, according to James 3:18, will sow peace. *"And the fruit of righteousness is sown in peace of them that make peace."*

A church member might ask his pastor, "Can I have the liberty to see something different than you?" The answer from God's Word is yes. Do you, the reader, have liberty to see something different than me—the author? Yes. For example, I like German chocolate cake, and you might like lemon meringue pie (more power to you). I am not a big lemon meringue pie eater. Now I would eat lemon meringue pie if I were to come to your house and you served it. I would even have a second piece. I did not say I hated lemon meringue pie. Just because your taste buds have not matured to the point of German chocolate cake, I am not going to be against you!

Now let me speak regarding church policy. Can a member have liberty to see something different than the pastor? I am a pastor, and I am going to shock you. Yes, a member has the liberty to see something different than the pastor, but that church member does not have liberty to live and speak with an intention to be divisive.

I was talking to a pastor about a month ago. He is the pastor of a much larger church than the church I pastor, and he is not a Baptist. We talked about some things in the Lord's work, and we had good fellowship in just talking about leadership.

At one point in our conversation I said, "You are not an independent Baptist, are you?"

He knew where I was coming from in that question, and he laughed and said, "I guess I'm not."

I said, "Let me ask you something. Did you ever have anyone in your church that just couldn't seem to follow leadership, or is it just us independent Baptists?"

He said, "Brother Chappell, let me help you with something."

I said, "Help me."

He said, "I probably do not have all the 'standards' that you have, but people are going to get crossways about the color of the carpet, where the ushers seat them, and how the parking lot flows. You just have to understand something; it is just in the heart of some people to be that way." In fact, some Christians today have become pathological antagonists. Their unkind ways are often carried out under the guise of Christian love and liberty.

Liberty is the privilege of obeying the Lord. It is not an excuse to act unkindly or ungodly to others. Liberty is not to be used as an occasion to the flesh.

Misinterpretation #2

"I can tempt my Christian brother to do wrong because I have liberty."

Another misinterpretation of liberty is that you can use the guise of liberty to tempt other believers to do something that they should not do. I have dealt with several cases when one Christian said to another, "We can sin and still be okay in the Christian life because we have liberty."

This mindset is a trick of the Devil, and it is an abuse of true liberty. Second Peter 2:18 refers to those who were professing faith in Christ, but in actuality they were false teachers. Verse 18 says, *"For when they speak great swelling words of vanity,* (Things like, "I have been saved for a long time. I have known God for a long time, so let me help you to further enjoy the Word of God so that you are not held down.") *they allure through the lusts of the flesh,* (They say things like, "You don't have to be so restricted; let's loosen up a little.") *through much wantonness* (loose living), *those that were clean escaped from them who live in error."* Verse 19 continues, *"While they promise them liberty, they themselves are the servants of corruption...."*

Picture a new Christian who is running his race in his newfound faith. He is running as hard as he can, and he is happy in his newfound liberty in Christ. Now picture someone who says to this new Christian, "If you really want to have some fun in the Christian life, don't run toward obedience." He will always tempt through the lust of the flesh.

Notice again verse 19 says, *"While they promise them liberty, they themselves are the servants of corruption…."* You had better beware of someone who is trying to get you to abuse your liberty.

For example, take two men on a construction job. Both are Christians, but one has a more liberal interpretation of the Scripture and a misinterpretation of liberty. When he sees his Christian co-worker going to church three times a week, he begins to fall under conviction about his own life because he basically lives a lukewarm Christian life. Many times this professing Christian will begin to allure with the lust of the flesh. He may say, "Hey, man, you don't have to be so serious about this thing; you don't have to be so involved."

Sadly, in this confrontation, the new Christian never gets the whole story right up front. What begins with just one small step turns out to be a country mile. Capture what 2 Peter 2:20 says, *"For if after they have escaped the pollutions of the world through the knowledge of the Lord and Saviour Jesus Christ, they are again entangled therein, and overcome, the latter end is worse with them than the beginning."*

Let us say, for example, that I meet a man while out door knocking and inviting people to church. After he expresses interest, I make an appointment to go back to his house and nurture a relationship with him. Finally, after working with him and praying for him, he decides to accept Christ as his Saviour. Not long after that, he begins coming to church and loving it! Through the preaching and teaching at church, he learns about a biblical Christian life.

The Bible says that people who misinterpret liberty will subtly try to entangle this man back into the life from which he was saved! Though he has escaped the pollutions of the world, they will try to allure him back into them. It grieves my heart to see other Christians come and say, "Hey, come back just a little bit to the entanglements of the world. You have liberty." They may not verbally express those words, but their heart attitude is saying, "You don't have to act so conservative. You can still be a good Christian and live like you used to live."

Let me be clear; your lifestyle will never change your standing with God. If you are truly saved, then positionally you are sanctified and sealed before a mighty God, and nothing can change that. But wait, there is such a thing as daily sanctification. It does matter to God how you live. He is very concerned with how we live our lives. My focus, as a pastor, is in helping people develop a heart for God. If I am working with a family and the Holy Spirit is working in their hearts in regard to their lifestyle, the last thing that family needs is one of their own Christian brothers trying to undo what God is doing in their hearts. We need to be on the same team. We need to applaud and encourage each other in growth and in living for God.

A lady in our church years ago used "liberty" as her favorite buzzword. Soon her lifestyle began to change to the point that alcohol and worldly entertainment ruined her marriage. My heart breaks for that family and for those they influenced. You see, nobody ever backslides by himself. I still see that lady from time to time around our town.

Friend, it makes me want to weep. Somebody sold her the bill of goods when it came to her Christian liberty. What she needed was real Bible liberty, which gives freedom to obey the Lord. She did not need a license to sin. She did not need a license to return to the pollutions she escaped.

Think about this; I exist to win people to the Lord and try to help them escape what Peter called the "pollutions of this world." I have committed my entire life to this cause. Friend, you do not want to stand before the Lord some day as a Christian who hindered a brother in his spiritual growth, even if it was unintentional. Be very careful about misinterpreting your liberty in Christ and abusing it by tempting other believers away from a committed life!

Misinterpretation #3

"I have liberty, even if it causes others to stumble."

Liberty is also abused when it becomes a stumbling block to a fellow Christian. First Corinthians 8:9 says, *"But take heed lest by any means this liberty of yours become a stumblingblock to them that are weak."* Until you understand this verse, you probably will not understand separation as an important part of the Christian life. There are times that a Christian should separate from something that may not be wrong simply because it may become a stumbling block to a weaker Christian. We must be careful that our churches, our activities, or our homes do not become stumbling blocks to those who may be struggling with particular problems.

Someone may ask me, "Pastor, do I have liberty to drink alcohol?" Yes, if your question is can you drink and still be saved. I believe I can prove scripturally that Christians should abstain from alcohol, period; but let us say for the sake of illustration that someone could prove that it is good to drink alcohol. I would still believe it would be wise to abstain from alcohol, so we would not become a stumbling block to the weak.

Over the years, we have worked through struggles, and prayed through battles with many of our church members. I have tried to understand their struggles and share in their victories. I have great joy to know that these same Christians are now helping newer Christians win some of the same battles they themselves fought years ago. Rather than using their liberty as a stumbling block in the life of a weaker Christian, they are using their true liberty to disciple others into a closer relationship with Christ. A pastor can have great peace of mind when he knows that his church members are not abusing their liberty by weakening new Christians. I want our stronger Christians to help our weaker ones so they do not get back into bondage. When Christians are misinterpreting their liberty, this sort of growth and discipleship cannot take place.

Let me illustrate. We have a full calendar of church activities. Every activity is planned to help Christians grow closer to the Lord and to help our church family grow closer together. One of our members might ask, "Do I have liberty to skip a men's activity or a ladies' activity and get some of my pals from the church and just do our own thing?" The answer would be yes. Every one of our members has the liberty to make that choice. However, when the pastor of a church is trying to bring people closer to the Lord, it is wrong for a member of that same church to set a direction which is in contradiction to the direction of the church.

That missed activity or message could be the very thing he needs in his Christian life!

Now please understand, I am not saying that every church member should attend every activity or church function. Obviously, due to work schedules, relatives, sickness, and other inconveniences, it is not possible to be at everything on the church calendar. I am simply saying that we should use our liberty to help others get to church, not away from it!

The Bible says, *"But take heed lest by any means this liberty of yours become a stumblingblock to them that are weak"* (1 Corinthians 8:9). For example, a Christian lady may have liberty to wear what she wants to wear, but I certainly would encourage her to remember the scriptural admonition for modesty in this area. *"In like manner also, that women adorn themselves in modest apparel, with shamefacedness and sobriety; not with broided hair, or gold, or pearls, or costly array"* (1 Timothy 2:9).

In our text, Paul is saying, do not use your liberty to cause someone who is weak to stumble. When a lady comes to sing on the platform of our church, she will be dressed modestly. This is not a legalistic statement, it is a leadership statement. There are churches across America saying, "We have liberty to wear halter tops and shorts to church and just worship the Lord." We have churches in our town that do that, and they do have liberty.

Some folks who think they are very strong are really very weak. The more you get into the Word of God, the more you see that you are not where you think you are. I do not say that to hurt you, because I find that to be true in my life. Sometimes when I think I really have arrived, I find out that I have a long way to go.

Paul says to take heed lest by any means you use your liberty and it becomes a stumbling block. There are many new Christians in our midst. They are observing us as their examples. We need to be careful that we do not inadvertently harm their spiritual growth. I do not think anyone purposely says, "I am going to be the stumbling block; that is my goal." The word *liberty* in 1 Corinthians 8:9 is the Greek word *exousia*. It means "the right which you assert." The Corinthians were asserting their rights at the expense of their responsibility as many Christians do today.

America has not been built by emphasizing our rights. Our nation has been built by emphasizing responsibility. We have a mission to accomplish. We are to win people to Jesus Christ, and to help them to grow in grace and into the image of Jesus Christ (2 Peter 3:18).

CHAPTER TEN

The Means of Liberty

We have seen the meaning of liberty and some of the misinterpretations of liberty. Now I want to show you the means of liberty, the way of enjoying liberty.

How can I understand and enjoy the means of liberty? We are going to see what real liberty is all about.

James 1:22–24 says, *"But be ye doers of the word, and not hearers only, deceiving your own selves. For if any be a hearer of the word, and not a doer, he is like unto a man beholding his natural face in a glass: For he beholdeth himself, and goeth his way, and straightway forgetteth what manner of man he was."*

In this chapter, we will see there is no true liberty for a Christian who violates the teachings of Scripture. God is calling for doers of the Word.

Verse 25 says, *"But whoso looketh into the perfect law of liberty, and continueth therein, he being not a forgetful hearer, but a doer of the work, this man shall be blessed in his deed."*

What really frustrates many of the folks who like to talk "liberty," is when you talk about the "law" of liberty. Do you know what the law of liberty is? It is the Bible. Therefore, understanding liberty and enjoying liberty comes only to a Christian who is obeying the Bible—the perfect law of liberty.

Jesus said in John 8:32, *"And ye shall know the truth, and the truth shall make you free."* I do not begrudge the fact that I cannot do certain things. I am glad that God has given me through His Word some discernment to avoid certain situations and certain places and conditions. I know that my Lord gives me guidelines for my protection, not to hurt me. I do not grumble at the Lord because He has told me to avoid the appearance of evil. I thank the Lord that He loves me and gives me these guidelines. You will begin to mature as a Christian when you begin to see old-fashioned preaching and Bible-based convictions as your best friend, not something that robs your joy.

The great British preacher, Dr. Foresight, said it this way, "The purpose of life is not to find your freedom; the purpose of life is to find your Master. When you find your Master, you will find your freedom."

The Bible says in John 1:14, *"And the Word was made flesh, and dwelt among us, (and we beheld his glory, the glory as of the only begotten of the Father,) full of grace and truth."* Jesus was Grace and Truth. He is the Truth; He is also Love. He is full of grace. He has a loving disposition. He has a forgiving heart, but He is full of truth. We can become unbalanced in grace by neglecting the truth. But if we are going to be like Jesus, we have to be full of both. We cannot neglect the truth of the Word of God which proclaims the holiness of God. We need a balance of grace and truth in order to be more like our Lord Jesus.

PART THREE

Separation—Why Is It Important?

CHAPTER ELEVEN

The Proper Approach to Separation

O ye Corinthians, our mouth is open unto you, our heart is enlarged. Ye are not straitened in us, but ye are straitened in your own bowels. Now for a recompence in the same, (I speak as unto my children,) be ye also enlarged. Be ye not unequally yoked together with unbelievers: for what fellowship hath righteousness with unrighteousness? and what communion hath light with darkness? And what concord hath Christ with Belial? or what part hath he that believeth with an infidel? And what agreement hath the temple of God with idols? for ye are the temple of the living God; as God hath said, I will dwell in them, and walk in them; and I will be their God, and they shall be my people. Wherefore come out from among them, and be ye separate, saith the Lord, and touch not the unclean thing; and I will receive you, And will be a Father unto you, and ye shall be my sons and daughters, saith the Lord Almighty. Having therefore these promises, dearly beloved, let us cleanse ourselves from all filthiness of the flesh and spirit, perfecting holiness in the fear of God.—2 Corinthians 6:11–7:1

Throughout the book of Second Corinthians the Apostle Paul defends and defines his ministry. He does not do this in an arrogant way. He does not do this in an egotistical sense of vaunting himself. Rather, under the inspiration of the Holy Spirit of God, the Apostle Paul helps some confused Christians to realize what his ministry had really been while in their midst.

Notice the heart of the apostle in 2 Corinthians 4:1–2, *"Therefore seeing we have this ministry, as we have received mercy, we faint not; But have renounced the hidden things of dishonesty, not walking in craftiness, nor handling the word of God deceitfully; but by manifestation of the truth commending ourselves to every man's conscience in the sight of God."* Paul's testimony clearly states, "Our ministry has been a ministry where we have renounced the hidden things of dishonesty. We are not like the false teachers of Corinth, but we have done our very best in giving the manifestation of truth, commending ourselves in the sight of every man's conscience." He is defending and defining his ministry.

Paul felt there must be a "manifestation of the truth" if the unsaved world would feel in their conscience a need for Christ. Many of today's Christians have so little outward manifestation of Christ. Thus, the lost world often senses no need in their heart (conscience) for Christ.

The reason for the doctrines of separation and holiness are found in 2 Corinthians 5:10–11, *"For we must all appear before the judgment seat of Christ; that every one may receive the things done in his body, according to that he hath done, whether it be good or bad. Knowing therefore the terror of the Lord, we persuade men; but we are made manifest unto God; and I trust also are made manifest in your consciences.*" Paul was convinced of the terror of the Lord. Grace had taught his heart to fear and respect God. I hope you have an awe for God in your heart as well. The same grace that cleanses a lost heart, also first causes a heart to "fear" or feel conviction. The same man who said, "The love of Christ constraineth me," also said, "The terror of the Lord persuadeth me."

Someone might wonder, why would the very apostle who brought these people to Christ have to explain such basic things? Why would the Apostle Paul have to come back to these people in a letter and explain to them the ministry, the motives of ministry, and his faithfulness in the ministry? Why would all of this have to be explained over and over again? The reason is very simple; the hearts of the Corinthian believers had been stolen away by false teachers. From the time that the church had been established until the time they received this letter, their hearts had been stolen away.

In 2 Corinthians 6:12, the Bible says, "*Ye are not straitened in us, but ye are straitened in your own bowels.*" This verse is saying, "We have not been withholding our love from you, but *you* have been withholding your love from us." They had become cool toward him. He was writing to them to set the record straight about ministry. These Corinthian believers had come under the influence of false teachers who had castigated the Apostle Paul. They had questioned his ministry. Because of what they had heard, their hearts had become very cold toward him. So he was writing to warm that friendship again.

Think of someone you knew, or thought you knew fairly well, with whom you had a good relationship. You greeted one another warmly. You were friends. Then one day your greeting was met with a cool response. Perhaps your friend just kind of turned and walked away as though maybe you were not there. You were sensing that something was different, that something was wrong. Similarly, Paul had sensed a change in his relationship with the Corinthian church.

The Call to Separation

Paul is writing to people who have been influenced to the point that they have cooled off in their fellowship with him. Now he is going to actually command them to separate themselves from those who have influenced them away from the faith. He is calling them to separation.

Four Preliminary Considerations

As we answer the question—"Why is separation important?"—there are four preliminary thoughts that I want to share with you.

1. Separation is a distinguishing doctrine of a truly fundamental church.
A church that is truly fundamental will not only preach and teach the whole Word of God, but will challenge people to

separate from organizations or worldly practices that would draw them away from the teachings of the Word of God. A fundamental church believes in and teaches separation from false doctrine and practice.

One of the distinguishing characteristics of a fundamental church is that it teaches and practices with a spirit of love this matter of separation from false teaching. Jude 3 says, *"Beloved, when I gave all diligence to write unto you of the common salvation, it was needful for me to write unto you, and exhort you that ye should earnestly contend for the faith which was once delivered unto the saints."* Many Christians have statements of belief, but rarely contend for them.

2. The primary goal of separation should always be that we are separated unto Christ.

The primary goal or the first matter in discussing separation is not, "What am I separating from?" but "Who am I separating unto?" When many people hear the Word preached, they think, "Oh boy, he's going to tell me where I can't go, who I can't be with, and what I can't do." When we put it first into the negative connotation, then we completely forget the positive reality that we are separating unto the Lord Jesus Christ. Paul said in Romans 1:1, *"Paul, a servant of Jesus Christ, called to be an apostle, separated unto the gospel of God."*

Someone might have come to Paul and said, "How could you, in your life, go without so many things? How could you suffer so many trials? How could you abstain from certain enjoyments when you had the liberty to go ahead and enjoy those things?" Paul said the reason that he could separate from certain things was because of the Person he had separated unto.

How can our missionaries live under such pressure? How can they separate themselves from this land filled with its amenities and blessings? It is because there was a day in their lives when they said, "Lord, I give You all of my life. I am separating myself unto You." Therefore the matter of separation involves, first of all, separating our hearts unto God.

A person who is yielded to God, according to Romans 12:1, will not rebel at this matter of separation from the world. *"I beseech you therefore, brethren, by the mercies of God, that ye present your bodies a living sacrifice, holy, acceptable unto God, which is your reasonable service."*

When I am separated unto God, it is not a big problem then to separate from the world; because the closer I get to God, the further away I am from the world.

The heart of the problem with so many Christians is a problem of the heart. When Christians are struggling with matters of separation from the wrong religious entities, oftentimes it is due to a heart problem.

The first issue is separation unto God. You and I need to ask this question right away, "Is my heart right with God? Is my heart given over to God, separated unto God?" Then, when someone teaches about being separated from the world, I am going to find it easier to understand. But if my heart is not yielded to God and someone is telling me I need to separate from a false religion or from a friend who is taking me down, then I am going to rebel. If my heart is first of all yielded to the Lord, I am going to understand these things and yield more easily.

3. The doctrine of separation is probably one of the most neglected doctrines in Christendom today.

Many churches are bringing the world's philosophies into the church. Consequently, when someone from another church background comes to a church like Lancaster Baptist Church, their immediate thought is, "Wow, these guys are out in left field, and they have all these old-fashioned ideas that no one has had in thirty years." It seems so strange to them.

New Christians do not usually think that way. New Christians usually think, "Oh, I always thought Christians shouldn't tattoo their bodies." It is always the folks who have become somewhat carnal in another church who have trouble with the doctrine of separation. They have been in a church where they became acclimated to the world to the point that Christ was not making a difference in their lives.

This doctrine of separation is very neglected, yet it is a doctrine that is taught in the Word of God. It needs to be taught in churches more and more if we are going to maintain the standard to be the salt and the light that Christ has called us to be in Matthew 5:13–16, *"Ye are the salt of the earth: but if the salt have lost his savour, wherewith shall it be salted? it is thenceforth good for nothing, but to be cast out, and to be trodden under foot of men. Ye are the light of the world. A city that is set on an hill cannot be hid. Neither do men light a candle, and put it under a bushel, but on a candlestick; and it giveth light unto all that are in the house. Let your light so shine before men, that they may see your good works, and glorify your Father which is in heaven."*

As more worldliness comes into the church, there are fewer distinguishing characteristics on the part of the church and in its message to the world.

4. The separated life is a Christ-like life.

The goal of Christian education and the goal of our Bible study is to develop the mind of Christ. We are not here to develop some kind of a humanistic philosophy to go out and have a good attitude and do our best in the flesh. I cannot do my best in the flesh and please God. We are here to develop the mind of Christ and live a separated life.

The Bible says in Hebrews 13:13, *"Let us go forth therefore unto him without the camp, bearing his reproach."* The reference is to the fact that Jesus Christ was crucified outside of the city. Jesus Christ was outside of the camp. The Bible challenges us to go to Christ and to be willing to bear His reproach.

Our flesh wants to be part of a large ecumenical movement because of the acceptance we find in it. Oftentimes we dress or act a certain way because, in doing so, we find acceptance. We do not want to be too different at work because we want to be accepted by our peers. We want to laugh a little at the wrong kind of jokes because we want to be accepted.

You see, our flesh does not want to bear reproach. Our flesh wants to be popular with everybody all the time. Would you admit that your flesh enjoys the accolades and acceptance of your peers? There is nothing wrong with acceptance as long as we do not compromise our biblical beliefs. The point is, if we are going to live a Christ-like life, it is going to involve taking a stand and bearing some reproach. *"Yea, and all that will live godly in Christ Jesus shall suffer persecution"* (2 Timothy 3:12).

I am praying that God would cause a new understanding of the doctrine of separation. Then we will come out and be separate because we know it is right and we want to be like Jesus Christ. I am praying that God will cause us to have a strong conviction to live for Him, not because the other people in the church are doing it or because it is required of leaders in the church, but because we want to be like Jesus Christ. That is a much higher motivation.

When it comes to the doctrine of separation, there is a tremendous need for balance, and I will quickly give you two ends of the scale. At one end of the scale are groups like the Amish people. They are incredibly separated. They are so separated that they live in a closed community. They have no desire even to do business or interact with outside people. To the Amish, everything is black or white; there are no grays. They do not even use motorized vehicles or other modern conveniences. I would say the right word would be "isolationists."

At the other end of the scale is the modern-day, evangelical type of churches that downplay the doctrine of separation. They say those who believe the doctrine of separation are legalists who do not understand grace. They have come to the place where they practice little or no separation. Their lives as Christians are often not distinguishable from the life of someone who is not saved. They often look the part, act the part, and talk the part of an unbeliever.

In the past few years I have witnessed the failure of strict rules without love and grace. I have also seen the failure of radical grace without adherence to truth. On the one hand, a high profile separatist Baptist pastor who often condemned others resigned his ministry because of his addiction to alcohol. On the other hand, a Christian church pastor and prolific author of many inspirational books recently submitted to a restoration plan given by his elders due to his alcoholism.

Please note that the teaching of separation is not dealing with contact, it is dealing with conformity. In other words, we are not saying that you should not have a friend who is not saved. How are we going to lead anybody to Christ if we cannot have friends who are unsaved? Every one of us comes in contact with unsaved people throughout the week. Praise God for that. We are not talking about isolationism. Sometimes people who want to be critical of a fundamental church say, "Oh, they're just sort of isolationists." That is not at all what our church believes. We believe that we are to be out there in the world, but we need to realize that we are not to conform to the world. We want our lives to make a difference and to have an effect on those around us and not vice versa.

CHAPTER TWELVE

Separation Is Important Because of Our Standing

Why is the doctrine of separation so important? It is important because of our standing as Christians. If you are saved, the Bible describes you as a child of the light. That is your standing in Christ.

Let us be reminded of 2 Corinthians 6:14, *"Be ye not unequally yoked together with unbelievers: for what fellowship hath righteousness with unrighteousness? and what communion hath light with darkness?"* Nearness is likeness. The Corinthians were influenced by some people of different faiths and different concepts. These friendships had begun to make an impact upon them to the point that they were looking down on the very man who had brought them to Christ. Though he was just a man, he was an apostle who loved them.

The Christian Has a Divine Nature

The Christian has a divine nature. The Bible teaches that when we are saved, the Holy Spirit of God takes up residence in our lives. We have a divine nature, and we have the old fleshly nature. Thank God that through the power of the Holy Spirit, we can have victory over that old fleshly nature.

Second Peter 1:4 says, *"Whereby are given unto us exceeding great and precious promises: that by these ye might be partakers of the divine nature, having escaped the corruption that is in the world through lust."* Here the Bible says that we are partakers of a divine nature. When you accepted Jesus Christ as Saviour, the Holy Spirit of God took up residence in your life. Because of that, you now have a divine nature. You have the Holy Spirit living within you. By the presence of the Holy Spirit in my life, I have the light of the Lord Jesus living in me. Therefore, I should not have fellowship with darkness. I am not to yoke together with someone whose spiritual nature is in opposition to Christ.

Second Corinthians 6:14 says, *"Be ye not unequally yoked together with unbelievers: for what fellowship hath righteousness with unrighteousness? and what communion hath light with darkness?"* A classic example of a yoke is that of two business partners. It is very difficult for a Christian who has an unsaved business partner to glorify God in that business, because the main goal of the unsaved partner is to make money. The partner has no desire to glorify God.

Where does this term unequal yoke come from? It comes from the Old Testament in Deuteronomy 22:10, *"Thou shalt not plow with an ox and an ass together."* In this passage, the Jews were told not to yoke together an ox and a donkey. The ox was considered a clean animal, and the donkey was considered an unclean animal. God said not to put them together, or they would never get the fields plowed. They had two opposite natures.

If you yoke yourself together with someone who has an opposite spiritual nature, he will normally drag you down or take you in another direction before you bring him to Christ. For example, I have had people tell me, "I'm just going to date this guy for a while. I know he's not saved, but my goal is to bring him closer to God and help him to be saved." It hardly ever works that way. Often, the person saying that is out of church within a few weeks. Why—because they violated a biblical principle and yoked together with an unbeliever.

Notice in 2 Corinthians 6:14–15 the terms "fellowship," "communion," and "concord:" *"Be ye not unequally yoked together with unbelievers: for what fellowship hath righteousness with unrighteousness? and what communion hath light with darkness? And what concord hath Christ with Belial? or what part hath he that believeth with an infidel?"* We need to recognize that there will be no fellowship, communion, or concord (harmony) with the Lord when we are trying to walk in the world.

If we try to walk in the world and with the Lord at the same time, that fellowship will be broken because we are being pulled in different directions. You may have a friend or a co-worker who pulls you in the wrong direction. That is why the Bible says, *"Be ye not unequally yoked…."*

The Divine Nature Is in Direct Opposition to an Unbelieving Nature

Someone with a divine nature is walking in the light, or at least he has the Holy Spirit in his life. Someone who has not been born again does not have the same inner impulse from God to do what is right. When you put them together as friends or in business, many times it is going to be nothing but warfare. Sometimes, it will take the man who is trying to walk with God away from the things of God.

A yoke is a type of harness. The farmer would take two animals and yoke them together underneath the harness. The animals, if they worked as a team, would get something done. They would really accomplish something. But if you yoke together two animals with different natures, you have a problem. They will try to go in different directions. It will be difficult for them to work as a team, and therefore they will get less accomplished.

We need to be careful about yoking together with the wrong crowd. This is what the Bible calls an unequal yoke. A believer with a non-believer is an unequal yoke. God says that because we are saved, our intimate relationships in life should be with believers.

Second Corinthians 6:15 says, *"And what concord hath Christ with Belial? or what part hath he that believeth with an infidel?"* Concord means harmony. What harmony hath Christ with Belial? Sometimes people say, "My friend is a Catholic. Can I go to his church? Can I go to the men's rally and pray with my Catholic friend or my Mormon friend? Is that okay if we all get together like that?" I think this verse answers the question. What harmony does someone who has Christ in his heart have with someone who is worshipping without the truth? I do not say this to be mean, but Roman Catholicism is a false system. It is a system of works. It is a system of idolatry. It is a system that enslaves rather than liberates.

The modern-day ecumenical movement is saying, "We want you fundamental, Bible-believing Christians to get together with these other groups that don't believe exactly as you do. Let us downplay doctrine. Put that doctrine of separation away. That is nothing. Put away that doctrine of eternal security. It is nothing." In our flesh that sounds great, doesn't it? We can be a part of the majority. That is what we always want. We want to be on the winning team. That is the way of American culture. The problem is, if it violates a biblical principle, then we cannot do it. Why? Because a fundamental Christian and those who hold a different doctrine are not going in the same direction.

The Bible is teaching us in verse 14 that because of my standing in Christ, I view my relationships in a totally different light. I am saved. I have the Spirit of God in my heart. I am standing in the light; and when things come my way, I need to ask some questions:

- Is that religious system of the light or of darkness?

- Is this friend who wants me to give him ten thousand dollars to be a business partner standing in the light or in darkness?

- Is this organization that my friend is encouraging me to be a part of spreading the light of Jesus?

- Is this a Christ-honoring opportunity or would this perhaps taint my testimony?

If you understand this principle of the unequal yoke, you will look at every relationship in the context of maintaining a stand for Christ that is distinctively honoring to Him.

CHAPTER THIRTEEN

Separation Is Important Because of the Scriptures

The doctrine of separation is important because of our standing as Christians. It is also important because of the Scriptures. Second Corinthians 6:16 says, *"And what agreement hath the temple of God with idols? for ye are the temple of the living God; as God hath said, I will dwell in them, and walk in them; and I will be their God, and they shall be my people."* We are the temple of the living God. A church building is not the temple. Your body and my body are the temple of the living God.

God says, "I want to be their God, and I want them to be My people." Our God is a jealous God. He is a possessive God. *"I am the LORD thy God, which have brought thee out of the land of Egypt, out of the house of bondage. Thou shalt have no other gods before me"* (Exodus 20:2–3).

God says, "I want you to be My people. I don't want you to be My people part of the time. I want you to be My people all the time."

If you will get that and understand it, you will see it is a tremendous compliment. The reason God tells us not to get involved in an unequal yoke is because He loves us and wants our fellowship.

Second Corinthians 6:17 says, "*Wherefore come out from among them, and be ye separate, saith the Lord, and touch not the unclean thing; and I will receive you.*" "Them" is speaking of those who are of the darkness, those who are of Belial, representing false religion, those who are unrighteous in their life, those who are unbelieving in their life. We are to "come out from among them." That means separation. We must believe in, understand, and uphold the doctrine of separation because it is a scriptural doctrine.

Come Out

There are several false lifestyles that we need to "come out from." Let us notice a few.

False Religions

Someone who is saved should not worship in a false religious system. A lot of times people say, "I know I'm saved, but do I really have to come out of that church?" I believe the Bible is very clear that if someone is saved, he has to come out of a false church. That is one of my major problems with most ecumenical evangelistic meetings. Often, if someone is saved in their meetings, he is encouraged to stay in an apostate church.

One of our deacons, Dan Migliore, came from a Catholic background. When Dan got saved at our church, we did not say, "Well, praise God, you're on your way to Heaven. Go on back now, keep those seven sacraments, and you might make it there." No. We said, "Dan, now that you are saved, you need to identify publicly with Christ; you need to come out and identify with a Bible-believing church."

Unsaved Companions

Secondly, if you have an unsaved companion and the Holy Spirit tells you he is taking you away from the Lord, then I believe the biblical commandment for you is to come out from among them. Take your stand before they take you down.

You say, "That's so negative. That's so hard. They gave me a loan of $500 back in 1962, when I was almost destitute. I know they say some bad words, and I know they drink around my kids, and I know they take God's name in vain, but they've been so dear to me." Wait a minute. If it is a negative influence on your family, you may need to make a tough decision.

I am not telling you not to go to your parent's house at Christmas time. I am telling you to stay in fellowship with your family. Love your unsaved parents. Love your unsaved grandparents. No matter how different their convictions are, they are your family; and though you are going to come out and be separate in the way that you live, you can never sever family ties. That is God's plan for your life. The Scriptures teach that through your loving and holy example, many of your family can be saved. You must, however, guard your heart in every relationship and be sure you are not adapting to the world, but conforming to the image of Christ.

Saved, but Worldly

I believe the Bible teaches that you are to come out from a relationship with someone who is saved but walking in darkness. This is one of the hardest things for people to understand. Until you understand this, you are not going to get the victory that God wants you to have in your life. The Bible says, come out.

Second Thessalonians 3:6 says, *"Now we command you, brethren, in the name of our Lord Jesus Christ, that ye **withdraw yourselves from every brother that walketh disorderly,** and not after the tradition which he received of us."* If a Christian is living a life that is contrary to what the Bible says, then the Bible teaches us to draw away from him.

Second Timothy 2:20 says, *"But in a great house there are not only vessels of gold and of silver, but also of wood and of earth; and some to honour, and some to dishonour."* I believe this passage can be applied to the church. I am not trying to discourage you, but in every church you have people who are gold and silver, and you have some people who are wood and earth.

Paul goes on to say in 2 Timothy 2:21, *"If a man therefore purge himself from these, he shall be a vessel unto honour, sanctified, and meet for the master's use, and prepared unto every good work."* I believe there comes a time in each of our lives where we will let go of a relationship that could pull us into a life, or an attitude, that is not pleasing unto the Lord

Jesus Christ. You need to let the Holy Spirit lead you in this area. God will give you the direction you need.

Some Christians today habitually gossip, and others are pathological antagonists toward churches or Christians with whom they disagree. A friendship with bitter Christians will derail you before you realize what is happening.

Be Ye Separate

The Bible says in 2 Corinthians 6:17, *"Wherefore come out from among them, and be ye separate, saith the Lord, and touch not the unclean thing; and I will receive you."* God wants us to come out from the world. He wants us to be separate unto Him and united with the Lord Jesus Christ. We are *in* the world, but we are not *of* the world. Our conversation is of another world. Our lifestyle should be pointed toward Heaven. We are to come out and be separate.

Touch Not the Unclean Thing

Verse 17 says, *"Wherefore come out from among them, and be ye separate, saith the Lord, **and touch not the unclean thing; and I will receive you.**"* The "unclean thing" was a reference to the idolatry of the day. I believe that the unclean thing is anything that demands my attention over Christ.

Maybe you have a few relics from your past life. God says, "Don't touch them. Don't leave it lying around. Don't leave all the old paraphernalia around. Don't touch the unclean thing. Don't let your old friend come into your house and think that there is still a possibility that he could get you to take drugs or engage in sin. Don't let your old friend come in and think there is the possibility that you would go to that wild party. Don't touch the unclean thing. Don't have something there that is not clean."

I am trying to be somewhat general so that you can apply this to your own situation. God says to come out. God says to be separate. God says, "Don't touch something that would defile your testimony."

When people see your life and your home, you want them to see that it is distinctively Christian—not perfect of course, but that it belongs to the Lord Jesus Christ. It is sanctified and set apart.

If we want the right testimony in our lives, we need to be separate in the following areas:

Be Separate in Our Affection

I need to be separate in the affections of my heart. That is where it all begins. Colossians 3:1-2 says, *"If ye then be risen with Christ, seek those things which are above, where Christ sitteth on the right hand of God. Set your affection on things above, not on things on the earth."*

If I am loving the Lord Jesus Christ with my whole heart, then obeying the Scriptures is simplified because it is from my heart. If I want to please the Lord Jesus Christ, I must be separate in my heart. Separation begins in your heart with your attitude toward God.

Be Separate in Our Works

Separation will continue as you separate from the world and from the works of this world. Titus 2:14 says, *"Who gave himself for us, that he might redeem us from all iniquity, and*

purify unto himself a peculiar people, zealous of good works."
Why did Jesus Christ die for you? So that He might redeem
you, and that He might purify you as a peculiar people.

Most people do not like to be peculiar. You will not go
to work tomorrow and say, "How can I be viewed as the
biggest jerk of the company? What can I do to set myself
apart as a peculiar person?" Peculiar is not what most of us
want to be. Most of us want to be accepted. God says that
He is going to redeem us and to set us apart to be peculiar
or different. As a child of God who believes in the doctrine
of separation, your life should be distinct.

CHAPTER FOURTEEN

Separation Is Important Because of God's Holiness

Why is the doctrine of separation important? First of all, because of our standing—we belong to the Lord Jesus Christ. Secondly, because of the Scriptures that tell us to come out and "be ye separate." Thirdly, the doctrine of separation is important because of God's holiness.

Second Corinthians 6:16 and 18 says, *"And what agreement hath the temple of God with idols? for ye are the temple of the living God; as God hath said, I will dwell in them, and walk in them; and I will be their God, and they shall be my people…And will be a Father unto you, and ye shall be my sons and daughters, saith the Lord Almighty."*

God says, "I don't want you to just be my child. I want to know you." He says, "When you come out of that old crowd, when you break that yoke, and when you come out of that false religion, then I can really be your Father, then I can know you in a special way."

Our God is a jealous God. Exodus 20:2 and 5 say, *"I am the LORD thy God, which have brought thee out of the land of Egypt, out of the house of bondage...Thou shalt not bow down thyself to them, nor serve them: for I the LORD thy God am a jealous God...."* God wants us to be separate unto Him. He wants all of our attention. Someone says, "Boy, the church wants all of my attention." No, it is far more important than that. God wants your attention. God wants you to have intimate fellowship with Him.

The Holy Spirit of God can be easily quenched. First Thessalonians 5:19 says, *"Quench not the Spirit."* God the Father and God the Holy Spirit are easily quenched. God says He wants to be our Father and He wants to have a relationship with us. But when we go back into wrong relationships or into wrong types of religions, God is quenched. Because He is holy, His desire for us is to be sanctified or set apart for Him.

God says, "I want to be your Father. I want to give you that acceptance you may have never known from an earthly father. I want to give you that love you may have never experienced from some earthly relationship. If you will come out from that false system, if you will come out from those wrong relationships, I will give you a friendship like you have never known."

Often, I think about Abraham. The Bible says, in Genesis 11:31–12:2, that Abraham separated himself from Ur of the Chaldees. He went toward a city that he had never seen, and he did it totally by faith. God was pleased when Abraham, by faith, separated himself and went off to follow God. *"And Terah took Abram his son, and Lot the son of Haran his son's son, and Sarai his daughter in law, his son Abram's wife; and they went forth with them from Ur of the Chaldees, to go into the land of Canaan; and they came unto Haran, and dwelt there. And the days of Terah were two hundred and five years: and Terah died in Haran. Now the* LORD *had said unto Abram, Get thee out of thy country, and from thy kindred, and from thy father's house, unto a land that I will shew thee: And I will make of thee a great nation, and I will bless thee, and make thy name great; and thou shalt be a blessing."*

In Genesis chapter 12, the Bible says that Abraham went into Egypt and backslid. God was not pleased. God wanted all of Abraham. God wanted Abraham to keep on following Him. God did not want Abraham to go into Egypt.

Likewise, we need to realize that God wants all of us. God does not want us to follow Him for a while and then go back into the old habits, back to the booze, or back to the old, wicked way of life. God wants us to be steadfast unto Him every step of the way.

Nehemiah 10:28 says, *"And the rest of the people, the priests, the Levites, the porters, the singers, the Nethinims,* **and all they that had separated themselves from the people of the lands unto the law of God,** *their wives, their sons, and their daughters, every one having knowledge, and having understanding."* After the wall around Jerusalem was finished, God asked His people to separate themselves unto him. That is what God wants us to do. He wants us to separate from the people of the lands, and He wants us to separate unto Him.

Again, we are not saying that we will not have unsaved friends or relatives. We will have unsaved friends. God wants us to be a light to them. We must not give our will, our emotions, and our full attention to them, but to Christ.

CHAPTER FIFTEEN

Principles, Convictions, and Standards

The question is, "Is the doctrine of separation important, or is it just some trumped up thing that fundamental, Bible-believing pastors just have to preach?" It is a Bible doctrine. It is important! Why?

First of all, it is important because of our standing. God says, "Because you have a divine nature, you cannot yoke together with someone of an opposite nature and still have success."

Secondly, it is important because of the Scriptures. The Bible says, "Come out and be separate."

Thirdly, it is important because of the sensitivity and holiness of our God. God says, "I don't want part of you; I want you to give Me your whole heart."

You might be thinking, "I can't please God." First of all, you are "accepted in the beloved." Through Christ, God is pleased. Additionally, the Bible says in 2 Timothy 2:4, "*No man that warreth entangleth himself with the affairs of this life; that he may please him who hath chosen him to be a soldier."*

You can please God. It is a choice. When we remember His grace and His love for us, we want to please Him. But beyond that, when God convicts you about something that is a hindrance in your fellowship with Him, do not become fatalistic and say, "Oh, I can never please God." Instead, allow God to change you.

Rather than saying, "I could never please God," let us say, "I'll never be perfect, but my goal is to be more like Jesus every day. That is my goal. I can't change everything overnight, but I am willing, Lord, day-by-day to change what You want me to change. I realize that You are a sensitive God, and I realize, Lord, that you desire my companionship. Lord, if there is any organization, if there's any person in my life that draws me away from You, I'm willing to separate, so that I can be closer to You." That should be your prayer. The goal is not separation. The goal is Jesus Christ.

Cleanse Ourselves

Second Corinthians 7:1 says, *"Having therefore these promises, dearly beloved, let us cleanse ourselves from all filthiness of the flesh and spirit, perfecting holiness in the fear of God."* What promises? If we will come out and be separate, He will be a Father to us. We will have an intimate relationship with Him. That is a promise!

If you want that closer relationship with God, He says, "Let us come out, dearly beloved, and cleanse ourselves from all filthiness of the flesh and of the spirit." You say, "How do I cleanse myself?" We can be cleansed through prayer and through the Word of God. We just spend time with the Lord, and that cleansing process begins.

James 1:27 says, *"Pure religion and undefiled before God and the Father is this, To visit the fatherless and widows in their affliction, and to keep himself unspotted from the world."* God's Word says that pure religion involves keeping ourselves unspotted from the world. You are not going to go home, get in your garage, climb under your car, change the oil, replace the spark plugs, and not get some grease on yourself. Likewise, you cannot be with a sinning crowd and not be affected by that crowd. We see that we are to cleanse ourselves.

James 4:4 says, *"Ye adulterers and adulteresses, know ye not that the friendship of the world is enmity with God? whosoever therefore will be a friend of the world is the enemy of God."* God says friendship with the world is enmity with God. God says when you yoke up with a wrong crowd, or you are laughing at those jokes, or you act the part of an unsaved man, you are acting as His enemy. You say, "Lord, I'm not your enemy. I'm saved. Lord, I love you." God loves you too, but He is telling you all the while, "Come out and be separate unto Me. Let us be intimate friends together." Christian friends, we need to realize that this doctrine of separation is vitally important if we are going to be close to the Lord Jesus Christ.

Sins of the Flesh versus Sins of the Spirit

Second Corinthians 7:1 says that we should, *"...cleanse ourselves from all filthiness of the flesh and spirit, perfecting holiness in the fear of God."* Notice the terms "flesh" and "spirit." Luke 15:11–32 gives the account of the prodigal son. The prodigal went out and committed the sins of the flesh. He left home with the money he had coming to him and partied all day long. He lived a riotous lifestyle. But he had to come back to that place where he repented. He went back to his father, and he said, "Father, I have sinned." The prodigal son was guilty of the sins of the flesh.

The rest of the story refers to the older brother, who thought, "I have been working the fields. I have been the faithful son, and now he comes home and gets the fatted calf and the diamond ring." He eyed his brother. That is what we would call the sin of the spirit.

Sins of the flesh are visible outwardly. Sins of the spirit are inward. God says if you want to be close with Him, you have to cleanse yourself of the sins of the flesh and the sins of the spirit.

Notice in 2 Corinthians 7:1, *"Having therefore these promises, dearly beloved, let us cleanse ourselves from all filthiness of the flesh and spirit, **perfecting holiness in the fear of God.**"* That means becoming like Jesus Christ. If you are perfecting holiness, you are becoming more like Jesus Christ. What was Jesus like? Compare the following two verses.

> *For such an high priest became us, who is holy, harmless, undefiled, separate from sinners, and made higher than the heavens.*—Hebrews 7:26

> *The Son of man is come eating and drinking; and ye say, Behold a gluttonous man, and a winebibber, a friend of publicans and sinners!*—Luke 7:34

In the book of Hebrews the Bible says that He is holy, and in Luke it says that He was a friend of sinners. Jesus Christ had contact without contamination. He is holy, but He is the friend of sinners.

Our goal should be to live a life that is distinct, clean, and right before God. But let us not shun the sinner. Let us not neglect having a friend who does not know the Lord. Our goal is to have contact with them but not to be contaminated by them.

Practical Application

Now let me help you practically with how to apply that principle in your life. We often hear the terms, "principle," "conviction," and "standard." Let me define them:

A **principle** is a Bible truth I must live by. A **conviction** is a personal belief based upon a Bible principle. A **standard** is a policy that helps me keep my conviction.

Let me illustrate this by giving you a principle, the corresponding conviction, and the standard that will result.

First of all, Malachi chapter 3 gives a principle that the tithe is the Lord's. It is a Bible principle I must live by, because the Bible says in Malachi 3:8-10, *"Will a man rob God? Yet ye have robbed me. But ye say, Wherein have we robbed thee? In tithes and offerings. Ye are cursed with a curse: for ye have robbed me, even this whole nation. Bring ye all the tithes into the storehouse, that there may be meat in mine house, and prove me now herewith, saith the LORD of hosts, if I will not open you the windows of heaven, and pour you out a blessing, that there shall not be room enough to receive it."*

Tithing is a Bible principle. Then from studying that Bible principle I have come to a conviction in my heart that a minimum of one tenth belongs to God.

I have, therefore, set some standards in my life that help me to maintain that conviction. I have standards in my life that I will write a weekly check to my local church for a minimum of ten percent. A standard is a policy that helps me keep my conviction.

Let me give another example of a principle. The book of First Corinthians clearly states that even nature itself teaches that a man should not have long hair. The principle is that a man should not have long hair. Based upon that Bible principle, I have a conviction that a man should not have long hair. To help me keep my conviction, I must have some kind of standard to help me understand or keep that conviction. In my life and in this ministry we have set a standard that a man's hair should be off the ear and off the collar. That is called a standard, and it is based upon a Bible principle.

How can you take a Bible principle, formulate a conviction, and then make it work in your life? First, you need to find some Bible principles, and then you need to allow God to turn those principles into your own convictions.

The Bible speaks about modest apparel. Is it something about which you need to be convicted? If it is, then you need to set some standards based on the biblical principle. You say, "Well, I'm not sure how to define modest apparel." Go home, look it up in the dictionary, and then ask the Lord, "Help me have the right kinds of convictions."

Philippians 4:8 says that I am to think about things that are pure and lovely. That is a Bible principle. Therefore,

I have a conviction that God wants me to govern my thoughts. My conviction is that I need to meditate on that which is right. To help me with my conviction, I need some standards. One of my standards which helps me with this conviction is that I will not watch movies with cursing or nudity.

You have a Bible principle, which leads you to a Bible conviction; then you set up a standard, which is a policy that helps you keep your conviction.

Now, you take someone who has no conviction, challenge them with a standard, and they will rebel every time. People without convictions will struggle with standards every time. But if you give some standards to help someone who already has convictions, he will be appreciative. *"Reprove not a scorner, lest he hate thee: rebuke a wise man, and he will love thee"* (Proverbs 9:8).

The Bible says in 1 Peter 1:13–15, *"Wherefore gird up the loins of your mind, be sober, and hope to the end for the grace that is to be brought unto you at the revelation of Jesus Christ; As obedient children, not fashioning yourselves according to the former lusts in your ignorance: But as he which hath called you is holy, so be ye holy in all manner of conversation."* Verse 14 emphasizes that you do not get saved and then try to look and act just like the world. Verse 15 explains the word "holy" means separated unto God.

We learn Bible principles, we gain Bible convictions, and then we establish Bible-based standards so that we can live a life more like the Lord Jesus Christ. That is basic Christianity. We need to realize it. We do not need to shirk it. We do not need to say, "I can't do it." God would never call us to a life that we could not live by His grace and by following His Word.

Is this matter of separation important? Yes, it is. Why—because of our standing, we have a new nature, we are saved now. Why—because of the Scriptures. The Scriptures say, "Come out and be separate." Why—because of God's nature. God says, "I want to be your Father, but I can't have that relationship with you if all those people over there are taking you away from Me." He does not want to share you with every other religion, with every other situation—God wants all of you.

The way we can practically apply this doctrine of separation is by studying the Word of God, finding Bible principles, developing Bible convictions, and then establishing standards to help us keep those convictions.

May God help us to be sensitive to His Word and His Spirit as we develop godly standards, by which our testimony may be clearly seen to a lost world.

PART FOUR

Conclusion

CHAPTER SIXTEEN

God's Replenishing Grace

*Thou therefore, my son, be strong in the grace
that is in Christ Jesus. And the things that thou
hast heard of me among many witnesses, the
same commit thou to faithful men, who shall be
able to teach others also. Thou therefore endure
hardness, as a good soldier of Jesus Christ. No
man that warreth entangleth himself with the
affairs of this life; that he may please him who
hath chosen him to be a soldier. And if a man
also strive for masteries, yet is he not crowned,
except he strive lawfully.*—2 Timothy 2:1-5

Recently, a little boy saw a commercial on television
for a particular type of detergent. As he watched the
commercial, it occurred to him that his cat needed a bath,
and this laundry detergent just might do the trick.

So, he went to the grocery store, grabbed some of the
detergent, and as he was going through the check-out line,

the grocer asked him, "What are you buying that soap for, son?" The boy said, "I'm going to give my cat a bath." The grocer replied, "That detergent is too strong for a cat, and if you give him a bath, it might kill him."

But the boy had watched the commercial and he knew better than the grocer, so he went home and used the detergent to give his cat a bath. A few days later, the same grocer happened to see him again in the store and asked, "Son, how's your cat?" The little boy matter of factly replied, "Well, he died."

Shaking his head, the grocer said, "Son, I told you that detergent was too strong. I told you that detergent would kill him." But the boy quickly answered, "Oh, mister, it wasn't the detergent that got him, it was the spin cycle."

Have you ever had a time in your life when you felt like you were stuck in the spin cycle? Have you ever had days or weeks when it seemed life kept spinning, one trial after another? We all have times in our lives when we need something far beyond our human strength to sustain us, restore us, and strengthen us for the journey ahead.

In the past chapters, we've seen that God's grace produces a lifestyle of godliness. We've seen that God's amazing grace will motivate us to live more holy and Christ-like on a daily basis. Yet, as we close this book, I want you to see just one more way that God's grace produces godliness and holiness in our lives—and that is by replenishing our strength when life seems to be stuck on the spin cycle! Friend, you can take great hope in the grace of God! This grace not only produces godliness within, but it also sustains us and gives us renewed strength to press forward into each new day!

In 2 Timothy 2, Paul was writing to a young man named Timothy. In fact, this is the last book that Paul ever wrote. As he wrote to this young pastor in training, you can sense that the Apostle Paul, whose death was drawing near, had a great desire to mentor and to prepare Timothy for what was inevitably going to come into his life and ministry. Paul knew that Timothy was in store for persecution, trials, disappointments, and all kinds of problems and spiritual battles. So, the aged apostle wrote to the young recruit and said to him, in verse one, *"Thou therefore, my son, be strong in the grace that is in Christ Jesus."*

Notice that Paul didn't say, "Timothy, be all that you can be." Nor did he say, "What the mind can conceive, you can achieve." He didn't say, "Timothy, just do your best." No, his best would not have been enough. Timothy needed God's divine anointing and strength. So Paul said, "Timothy, be strong in the grace that is in Christ Jesus."

Sometimes you'll come to a place in your life when you are at the end of your rope. You'll come to a place where you are at the end of your resources and out of strength. We all reach these moments of depletion, and it is in these moments when God says, "My grace is sufficient for you."

His Grace Replenishes Our Strength

Grace for Serving

Oftentimes, when we get busy with work, overtime, errands, children, and all the things that need to be done, the first things we begin to take out of our schedules involves our service to the Lord—things like church attendance, teaching a Sunday school class, going to a Bible study, reaching out to an elderly person, or being a blessing to someone in need. We often use the excuse that we just don't have the time or energy to continue doing these things.

Friend, this is why Paul wrote this command to Timothy. He knew Timothy would be tempted to stop serving God when his strength began to fail.

The word *strong* in this verse means "to be enabled." God says, "My grace is an enabling grace." When you don't feel able, God will energize you and make you able to do His will. In the context of verse two, serving Him meant teaching others and sharing the Gospel of Jesus Christ. So, grace is an all inclusive word for the power, inner working, and gifts of the Holy Spirit that enable you to serve God effectively.

God simply says, "If you will be strong in My grace, you can get it all done. You can do the work that I have called you to do." In Hebrews 12:28 the Bible says, *"Wherefore we receiving a kingdom which cannot be moved, let us have grace, whereby we may serve God acceptably with reverence and godly fear."* God tells us that we need grace to serve Him. We need strength to endure the hardness, evil, and trials that will come into our lives. James 5:10 says, *"Take, my brethren, the prophets, who have spoken in the name of the Lord, for an example of suffering affliction, and of patience."*

Supreme Court Justice Antonin Scalia recently said, "A Christian who attempts to live according to the Bible will be deemed as a fool in this society." In other words, if you are going to actually live out what the Bible says—at work, in your home and in your neighborhood—there will be some people who think you are out of step. They may even say things to persecute you. What is God's promise to you in those times? "I have strength for you! I can give you grace to continue serving Me."

Grace for Suffering

Sometimes we need strength just to go another day in our busy routine. But other times we need strength because of an extraordinary burden that we were not expecting. Our tendency in these unexpected times is to draw back in fear and doubt. We want to ask "Why? What is going on with this sickness that has come into our family? How in the world did we come to the place where our child is in juvenile hall? Why did I get the pink slip?"

The Devil tempts us to throw up our hands in despair and desperation and cry out, "I don't understand this!"

Someone once said, "Worry pulls tomorrow's clouds over today's sunshine." When you live in fear and worry, every day is cloudy! In my years as a pastor, I have seen Christians who have faced unbelievable circumstances and tragic news with a strength that could only be from God. In fact, in 2 Timothy 1:7, the Bible says, *"...God hath not given us the spirit of fear; but of power...."* The word for *power* in the Greek language is the word *dunamis* from which we derive the English word "dynamite." God says, "I am not giving you the spirit of fear. I am giving you the spirit of power. I am going to give you My power and My ability from the inside. I'm going to work in your heart so you can go forward and do what I have called you to do in living the Christian life." When we are fearful or facing a trial, God says, "I want to instill My power in your life."

As a family, one of our customs during the holidays is to take some time to be a blessing to others. Instead of thinking about what we get and how much we can eat, over the years we have visited people in rescue missions, rest homes, or hospitals, and tried as a family to minister to their needs.

A few years ago, on Thanksgiving Day, we went to the local hospital to visit one of our church members who was very sick. As we visited with him, we sang some of his favorite hymns, and I read the Scriptures. We were simply trying to be a blessing to him during his time of suffering.

After a few moments, he asked for his Bible and began to read verses to us that had come to mean much to him. Over the next several minutes as he shared Scripture and words of encouragement with us, I realized that I was seeing God's powerful grace working in the life of a suffering man. Though his body was weak with sickness, his faith was dynamite faith. God had put a power within him that was only from the Spirit of God.

When we are fearful, God says, "I want to give you power, love, and a sound mind." Then, when we are weary, God says, "I want to give you strength." Second Corinthians 4:16 is a verse from which I have often drawn strength, and it has been a blessing to me. It says, *"For which cause we faint not; but though our outward man perish, yet the inward man is renewed day by day."*

Do you ever have a day when you are just completely tuckered out? The body in which you live says, "Hey, bud, pull over. There's a rest stop. We need to spend some time there." Sometimes the outward man perishes, but, notice that God says, *"Yet the inward man is renewed day by day."* We can be replenished daily by the grace of God!

Christian, rejoice that you are more than just a body. You are a living soul whom God has created. God loves you and wants to encourage your heart from within. When you are weary, He wants you to have the strength that He, and He alone, can give.

I heard of a father and son who were shopping at the grocery store. The dad gave the son one of those little shopping baskets to carry their items. After a while, the basket began to fill up and the little fellow was leaning over a little bit with the load. A lady passed by, noticed the boy and said, "Son, that's a pretty heavy load for a little guy like you, isn't it?" He looked up at the lady with a resolute smile and said, "Oh, don't worry, ma'am, my dad knows how much I can carry."

I'm glad I have a Father in Heaven Who knows how much I can carry. I'm glad that He gives me grace and strength when the load seems a little heavy.

His Grace Replenishes Our Spirit

Have you ever noticed that even Christian people through years of trials, overtime, and raising families can become negative and critical in their spirits? Oftentimes I have seen the most joyful and positive spirit become depleted, downtrodden, and even hurtful. I believe the greatest thing we need in our homes and churches is a spirit that is right with God and joyfully anticipating God by faith.

When I was in high school, the cheerleaders did a little cheer at our basketball games that asked the other team a question. It went like this: "We've got spirit; yes, we do! We've got spirit! How about you?" Friend, I want to ask you,

"How about you? How is your spirit toward the things of God...toward the people of God...toward the church, the pastor, or the person across the auditorium from you?"

Many Christians feel as though they have been "burned." They carry some past hurt or offense as though it were a present reality every day of their lives. This condition is always destructive to their spirits.

With other Christians it may not be an offense as much as a general weariness with the daily spiritual battle. They feel they have been at this Christian life for a long time and a lethargy or weariness begins to overtake their spirits.

Friend, regardless of the reason your spirit is being tested, God wants to replenish your spirit. He doesn't want you to go through life grumpy, irritated, frustrated, and critical. He wants to create within you a right heart, a joyful spirit, and a grace-filled attitude.

He replenishes us from doubt to faith

Philemon was a Christian man in the first century who had been led to Christ by the Apostle Paul. He had a servant named Onesimus. Onesimus had run away from Philemon and had created an apparent breach in their relationship.

One day, in prison, he met the Apostle Paul, and there the Apostle led him to Christ. Paul then wrote a letter to Philemon on behalf of Onesimus. In that letter, Paul said to Philemon in verses 18 and 19, *"If he hath wronged thee, or oweth thee ought, put that on mine account; I Paul have written it with mine own hand, I will repay it: albeit I do not say to thee how thou owest unto me even thine own self besides."*
He was saying, "Now, Philemon, I'm the one who led you to

the Lord, so remember that when you are considering the forgiveness of Onesimus."

Then he said in verse 25, *"The grace of our Lord Jesus Christ be with your spirit. Amen."* He said, "Philemon, I know that Onesimus hurt you, but I am praying that the grace of our Lord Jesus Christ will be with your spirit. Don't let your spirit reflect that hurt. Don't let your spirit contain a bitterness toward Onesimus. May the grace of God be with your spirit."

Friend, God's grace can help your spirit today! His grace can take you from a place of doubt and questioning to a place of faith. Just as God wanted Philemon to believe in the salvation and transformation of Onesimus, God wants you to let His grace transform a doubting or suspicious spirit into a spirit of faith and trust in God.

He replenishes us from discouragement to hope

God wants to take our discouraged spirits and transform them into hopeful spirits. He wants us to rest in knowing that He is working on our behalf.

Notice what the Bible says in 2 Thessalonians 2:16–17, *"Now our Lord Jesus Christ himself, and God, even our Father, which hath loved us, and hath given us everlasting consolation and good hope through grace, Comfort your hearts, and stablish you in every good word and work."* God said, "I want you to know that you have hope because of My grace. You have comfort, can do every good work, and say every good word because of My grace." When there is sickness, you can have a good word. When there is a trial in your family, you can still have a good word and work through God's grace.

Nothing humbles me more than to visit someone struggling with cancer and have him say to me, "I know God is at work in my life. I know God has a reason for this." Nothing exhibits God any more than hearing someone in that valley say, "I know that God is with me. The Lord is my Shepherd and yea, though I walk through the valley of the shadow of death, God is with me…He's leading me to the still waters and to the green pastures." In moments like this, truly God is replenishing the spirit and giving strength that only He can give.

His Grace Will Replenish Our Supply

I don't know about you, but at our house, with a twenty-one year old son and a fifteen year old son, we go through groceries like cattle grazing at our house. I mean, the supplies run out fast. They don't just have a glass of milk, they have a half gallon of milk. It seems we have to re-supply constantly just to keep up with the fast rate of depletion!

That's somewhat how our Christian lives are. It often seems that our strength is constantly running out and our spirit is constantly being diminished. This is the nature of the spiritual battle that we wage from day to day, and we've seen that God's grace will restore and renew us from within.

Yet, there is one final way that God's grace works on our behalf. He wants to supply our needs. Every Christian faces spiritual and physical needs for which God wants to provide abundantly!

He supplies forgiveness

Friend, the greatest need you have ever had was forgiveness by God's grace. God knew your greatest need was not economic, educational, or entertainment. God said, "Your greatest need is that you might have the forgiveness of sin, and by My grace, I am going to meet that need through My Son, Jesus Christ." Though we don't deserve this forgiveness, God provides it freely to all who will accept it.

Ephesians 2:8-9 says, *"For by grace are ye saved through faith; and that not of yourselves: it is the gift of God: Not of works, lest any man should boast."* Here we are reminded that we didn't deserve to go to Heaven. Why? The Bible says in Romans 3:23, *"For all have sinned, and come short of the glory of God;"* In Romans 5:12, the Bible says, *"Wherefore, as by one man sin entered into the world, and death by sin; and so death passed upon all men, for that all have sinned:"*

In summary, we were born with a spiritual death sentence. We were born separated from God because of the sin that had come into the human race. Yet God looked at us, as sinful people, and said, "I love them and I want to exhibit grace toward them by offering forgiveness. I will pay for their forgiveness by dying on the Cross and shedding My blood for their sin."

The forgiveness that Christ offers allows God's righteous demand for a sin payment to be met. That is why Jesus is the only One Who can offer forgiveness.

Many religions and churches are filled with works for salvation. In other words, every false religion has a system of earning salvation. The lists vary from religion to religion, but the bottom line is the same…"If you do this, and this, and this, and this, you can be saved." Some religions go so far as to have people work for the salvation of others—deceased relatives, etc.

Simply put, these religions are directly opposed to the relationship of grace that God describes in His Word! The Bible clearly says we are not saved by "doing things," but rather we are saved by believing in Jesus Christ. We are saved by accepting what Jesus did on the Cross as God's gracious gift of salvation towards us.

There is a cemetery not far from New York City with a gravestone that has just one word on it. It doesn't have the name of the person, or his birth or death date. It doesn't have any family lineage or even a eulogy. It only has one word on it—*Forgiven*. That's the single greatest need you have, and it's the single greatest thing that could ever be said about you.

There was a little boy standing outside of Buckingham Palace who wanted to go in and see the king. Oh, how he wanted to see what it was like inside. He tried to get through a few times, but the guard said, "Stop, son," rebuffed him and put him back.

As he stood there crying, a man came by and said, "Son, why are you crying?" He said, "I want to go see the king." To that, the man put out his hand, and the little boy reached out and took it. Together they walked right past the guards and right into the throne room of the king. What a wonderful experience that must have been. Little did that boy know that he had put his hand into the hand of the Prince of Wales. His access to the throne room was granted because of the hand he was holding!

Much like that boy, I was unable to enter God's presence because of my sin. Yet, He sent His Son, the Lord

Jesus Christ, and extended His hand of grace to me when He died on the Cross. When I trusted Jesus as my Saviour, I placed my hand into His, and He has given me full access to the Heavenly Father by His grace! I can now go directly into the throne room of God and have a relationship with Him.

He supplies help

Sometimes the Lord calms the storm, and sometimes He lets the storm rage and He calms His child. God wants you to know that when the storm comes into your life, He is going to give you the help you need.

Some of my favorite verses are found in Hebrews 4:14–16, *"Seeing then that we have a great high priest, that is passed into the heavens, Jesus the Son of God, let us hold fast our profession. For we have not an high priest which cannot be touched with the feeling of our infirmities; but was in all points tempted like as we are, yet without sin. Let us therefore come boldly unto the throne of grace, that we may obtain mercy and find grace to help in time of need."*

God says, "When you need help, I have grace to help. I have a dynamite kind of power that will work on your behalf! I will release My Spirit's strength into your spirit. When you need grace to help in your time of need, I will give it to you." Grace is that by which the soul is supported in every trial and heartache of life.

A young boy had a shoe box in his home. Inside the shoe box he had some grass and twigs, and right in the middle, he had the cocoon of a moth. He was a curious boy and couldn't wait until that cocoon opened and the moth would come out. Day by day he watched, and finally saw a little opening in the cocoon. He looked inside and saw some bright orange color and knew the time was coming.

Over the next few hours he sensed there was a real struggle going on inside the cocoon, so he reached down and carefully widened the opening to help the moth out. After a moment the little boy noticed that the moth's wings were all shriveled up and unusable. Something was wrong.

The boy had not realized that the struggle of the moth was necessary for the muscle system of the moth to develop. In his attempt to relieve the struggle, he had crippled the future of the creature.

Sometimes, when we go through trials, we want to quit church, quit on our families, or we just want to pull over and quit on life. Yet, God allowed that trial so that we might exercise our faith in Him. He allowed the struggle that we might grow in grace and bring more glory to Him. Oh that we would recognize that the great need of our lives is not for God to take every problem away, but that we might have God's grace and power working in us through our struggles!

God says, "Be strong in My grace." Paul said, "Timothy, be strong in the grace that is in Christ Jesus." God's grace will replenish your strength. God's grace will take a bad spirit and make it better. God's grace will supply your need for forgiveness and help in time of need. God's grace will supply your need for strength and comfort during the trials of life. May God help us to grow in the grace of our Lord Jesus Christ and to be strong in His grace until He comes again!

May God bless you richly as you press forward on your journey to allow His amazing grace to produce a godly life that flows from within!

Notes

Chapter One
1.   J. Vernon McGee, *Thru the Bible with J. Vernon McGee: Matthew–Romans* (Nashville: Thomas Nelson, 1983).
2.   Dr. Ernest Pickering, *Are Fundamentalists Legalists?* (Decatur, AL: Baptist World Mission, 1994), p. 1.

Chapter Three
3.   Pickering, *Are Fundamentalists Legalists?*, p. 8
4.   Ibid.
5.   Ibid.
6.   Ibid.

Chapter Four
7.   A Leadership Forum, *Leadership*, "God, Money, and the Pastor," Fall 2002. Vol. 24, Number 4, p. 26.
8.   Pickering, *Are Fundamentalists Legalists?*, p. 36

Chapter Six

9. Josh McDowell, *How to be a Hero to Your Kids* (Dallas: Word Publishing, 1991), p. 25.

10. J. Oswald Sanders, *Spiritual Leadership*, Second Revision (Chicago: Moody Press, 1967), p. 29.

11. John R. Rice, *Bible Giants Tested* (Murfreesboro, Tennessee: Sword of the Lord Publishers, 1962), p. 164.

12. John W. Kennedy, *Christianity Today*, "Jerry Falwell's Uncertain Legacy," December 9, 1996, Vol. 40, Number 14, p. 63.

13. Ibid.

14. Tommy Barnett, *There's a Miracle in Your House: God's Solution Starts With What You Have*, (Orlando: Creation House Press, 1993), p. 84.

15. Charles Stanley, *The Source of My Strength*, (Nashville: Thomas Nelson Publishers, 1994), p. 223.

16. Paul Chappell, *Guided by Grace*, (Murfreesboro, Tennessee: Sword of the Lord Publishers, 2000), pp. 48–60.

Chapter Eight

17. Jack Gordon, *LADC Star*, "Skunk Works Pride," April 28, 1995

About the Author

 Dr. Paul Chappell is the senior pastor of Lancaster Baptist Church and the president of West Coast Baptist College in Lancaster, California. He is a powerful preacher of God's Word and a passionate servant to God's people. He enjoys spending time with his family, and he loves serving the Lord shoulder to shoulder with a wonderful church family.

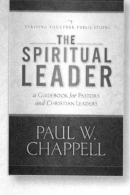

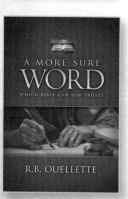

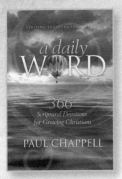

a breath of fresh air—
delivered monthly

spiritual leadership moment
a monthly downloadable lesson subscription from Dr. Paul Chappell

This subscription brings fresh ideas, encouragement, and ministry insight to your inbox every month! You receive the audio file in mp3 format, lesson outline, along with permission to use the lessons in your own ministry.

These lessons are perfect for staff meetings, lay-leadership development, or personal growth.

The monthly subscription is a $9.95 recurring monthly charge.

More than seventy past lessons are also available for $9.95 each. (Hear a sample lesson at strivingtogether.com.)

- **a spiritual leadership lesson**
- **a lesson outline**
- **permission for use**
- **helpful staff training lessons**
- **personal growth helps**
- **bonus mp3s and mailings**
- **special discount offers**
- **annual lunch with Dr. Chappell**
- **$9.95 per month**

subscribe today at strivingtogether.com!

Visit us online

strivingtogether.com

dailyintheword.org

wcbc.edu

lancasterbaptist.org

paulchappell.com